Essential Holistic Therapies

Eagle Editions

AN OCEANA BOOK

Published by Eagle Editions Ltd
11 Heathfield
Royston
Hertfordshire SG8 5BW

This edition printed 2002

ISBN 1-86160-447-5

QUMEHT

This book is produced by
Quantum Publishing Ltd
6 Blundell Street
London N7 9BH

Manufactured in Singapore by
Universal Graphics Pte Ltd

Printed in Singapore by
Star Standard Industries Pte Ltd

CONTENTS

AROMATHERAPY

ANNA SELBY

INTRODUCTION

Aromatherapy is, as its name suggests, a therapy that uses aromas. These aromas are produced from many different plants – flowers, trees and herbs – and from various parts of those plants – roots, leaves, flowers, bark and rind. The volatile essential oil of the plant (including its odour) – often referred to as the plant's "life-force" – is captured through a process of extraction or distillation. Using plants for healing is, of course, a practice that began with our most distant ancestors, who ate them, made infusions to drink or applied them to the skin. They were also burned as incense in rituals and, in ancient Egypt, Greece and Rome, fragrances from plants (though not actual distilled essences) were used for medicinal and cosmetic purposes and very highly valued.

The essences of such plants as eucalyptus, rosemary and geranium are extracted for use as aromatherapy oils.

When the tomb of Tutankhamun was opened in 1922, there was still a lingering fragrance of frankincense from the pots placed there over 3000 years before. And, of course, frankincense and myrrh – which produce two of the most powerful essences in common use – were offered by the Magi, the three wise men, to the infant Jesus. This gives some measure of the value given them in the ancient world.

The distillation of essential oils, as now known, however, is thought to have been discovered in the late tenth century by the Arab physician known in the West as Avicenna. The process was brought back to the West by the Crusaders and applied to our native plants. Although the use of essential oils as a therapy flourished for a while, it had virtually disappeared by the beginning of the twentieth century. Then in the 1920s, René-Maurice Gattefosse, a French chemist, became interested in essential oils and discovered that not only were they powerful antiseptics, they also had remarkable healing powers. He learned this from personal experience. When his hand was severely burned in an experiment in his laboratory, he

person (mind, body and spirit) rather than mere symptoms, using non-invasive, natural techniques, and taking responsibility for our own health. Obviously aromatherapy very much embodies all these principles.

Although the oils can be used in a wide variety of ways, aromatherapy is very much linked with massage. A massage from a skilled aromatherapist is a real treat and deeply relaxing – making a good antidote to the high levels of stress that abound today. Depending upon the blend of oils used, the massage can also affect specific problems (see pages 40-61), as diverse as headaches and menstrual cramps, a sports injury or indigestion. A massage with essential oils also involves the use of both of the pathways into the body that they can take – via the skin and via the olfactory system.

In ancient Egypt plant extracts were used as medicine, cosmetics and for ritual purposes.

plunged it into neat lavender oil. Not only did it heal remarkably quickly, there was no infection and no scar. Hardly surprisingly, he continued his investigations and in 1928 wrote the book that coined the name the therapy has been known by ever since, *Aromathérapie*.

The first English book on the subject, *The Art of Aromatherapy*, by Robert Tisserand, was not published until 1977 and it is only since then that interest in aromatherapy has really begun to flourish in the UK. Since then, aromatherapy has played a major part in the remarkable resurgence of natural medicine. Holistic medicine has its emphasis on treating the whole

The distillation of essential oils is believed to have started with the Arab physician, Avicenna. The process was brought back to the West by the Crusaders.

Aromatherapy oils have the ability to affect our moods and fill a whole room with their fragrance on a simple burner.

The Olfactory System

The sense of smell is today undervalued to the extent that it is generally regarded as the least of the senses. Yet research has shown that people respond to smell on an emotional level more strongly than to the other senses. A scent can trigger a whole string of half-forgotten memories – the area of the brain associated with smell is the same as that of the memory. Certain oils also have a remarkable ability to transform and balance our emotions – relieving anxiety, depression or mental fatigue.

It is thought that the effect of smell is so strong and so immediate because the olfactory nerve is in direct contact with the limbic system, the emotional centre of the brain. The olfactory nerve cells terminate in the cilia, the tiny hairs in the nasal cavity. Their response to the stimulus of an aroma is to transmit a direct impulse to that part of the brain where the memory and emotions lie and connect to the hypothalamus and the pituitary gland that governs our hormonal systems. While a great deal more research on how the sense of smell works is still needed, there can be little doubt that its effect on both mind and body is profound.

Skin Absorption

During massage, when essential oils are dissolved in a carrier oil (or in the bath when they are dissolved in water), they can be absorbed through the skin via the hair follicles into the bloodstream or lymphatic system and then circulated throughout the body. The oils have a generally stabilizing effect on the body: lowering high blood pressure, stimulating sluggish circulation, and promoting detoxification and healthy cell renewal. (For the therapeutic actions of specific oils, see pages 11-21).

How to get Started

This book is primarily about self-help – but see page 62 for information on consulting a professional aromatherapist. You can buy the oils from reputable health shops or via mail order (page 63). It is important to realize that these oils are very potent. Use them only in the dilutions given in this book and remember to check the warning list of oils to avoid in various circumstances (page 41). This is particularly necessary if you are pregnant or using the oils on babies or children.

Never try to treat serious conditions yourself. Essential oils have their limitations and you should always consult a qualified medical practitioner if you think you have any cause for concern.

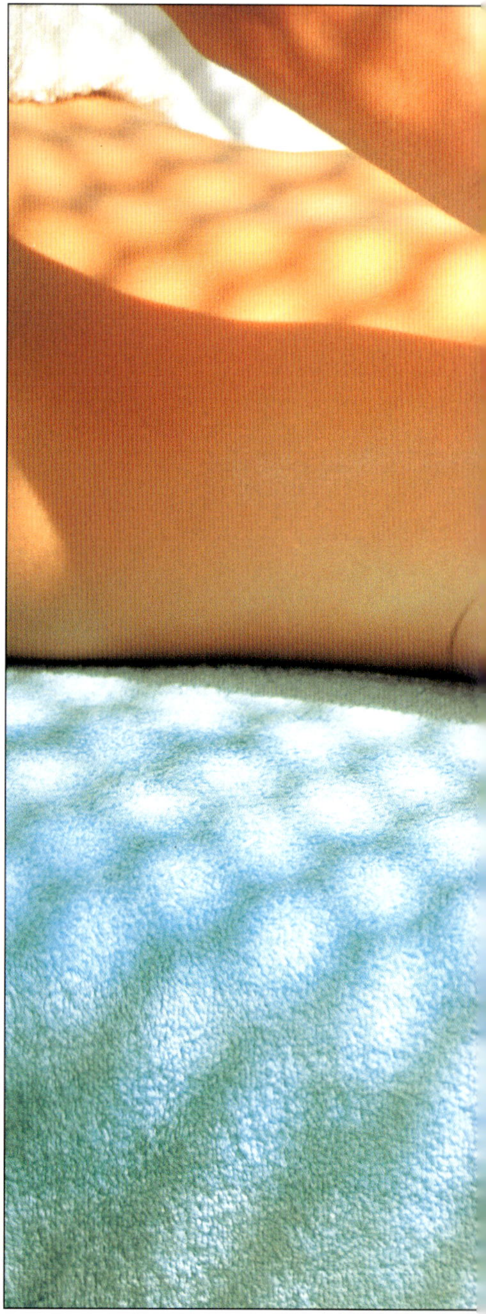

An aromatherapy massage is deeply relaxing, and the oils can penetrate the body both through the skin and by inhalation via the olfactory system.

THE ESSENTIAL OILS

The essential oils used in aromatherapy come from a wide variety of natural sources — herbs, flowers, leaves, wood, resin, seeds, fruit rind, roots and gum. They are extracted using a number of methods, often by steam distillation, to form a pure, highly volatile oil. There are other oils on the market, often described as "scented with essential oils" and these are definitely not to be confused with the real thing. True essential oils are undiluted and come in small (10ml) dark blue or brown bottles.

Aromatherapy oils can be used on many levels — physical, emotional, mental and spiritual — whether on their own, simply inhaled from a tissue or in conjunction with other therapies. It is important to dilute them before use (see dilution chart on page 24).

WARNING

- Except in the rare instances specifically mentioned in this book, essential oils should not be taken internally or applied undiluted directly to the skin.
- Citrus oils — bergamot, lemon, orange, mandarin and so on — should never be used on the skin before exposure to the sun as they may cause irritation.
- Keep oils out of the reach of children and, if they are accidentally swallowed, do not induce vomiting, but seek urgent medical help.
- There are several contra-indications to be considered (see the box on page 41 before using any oils).

There are several essential oils boxes on the market in which to store your oils. Alternatively, you can keep them in the fridge with their tops tightly sealed (or they may scent the food).

Relaxing Starter Pack

Aromatherapy oils are perhaps best known for their powers to balance and lift the spirits. These euphoric essences can be effective for all sorts of emotional problems, from stress and fatigue to depression and premenstrual tension (PMT). There are a number of ways they can be used for such treatments, but probably the best is as a full body massage (see pages 26-39). They can also be used as room scents on vaporizers, in the bath or simply inhaled from pillow or a tissue. The 11 essences listed here are those most readily available and easy to use. Other oils that can be used in this category are peppermint and bergamot (see pages 15 and 18), melissa, patchouli and orange (see pages 19-21).

Ylang-ylang *(above)*
(Cananga odorata)
Distilled from the flowers of the tropical ylang-ylang tree, this heady oil is renowned as an antidepressant and aphrodisiac. Its sweet, exotic scent makes it a popular ingredient in many perfumes, but it can be quite overpowering – only a few drops should be used in a blend with other oils, particularly jasmine, bergamot, and rose, as the strong scent may otherwise cause a headache.

Neroli
(Citrus aurantium)
This oil is also known as orange blossom and it is extracted from the flowers of the orange tree (see also Orange and Petitgrain). Like rose, it is both one of the most expensive oils and one of the most feminine. It is both calming and uplifting and very valuable as an antidepressant, especially in cases of nervous tension, extreme anxiety, hysteria and shock. It also has a generally calming effect on the heart and is good for palpitations. It combines well with woody and other floral essences.
Other uses: Insomnia; most skin conditions; as a facial toner, especially for mature skin.

Clary sage *(left)*
(Salvia sclarea)
Clary sage is not to be confused with sage, which is a more toxic essential oil best left to professional aromatherapists. Clary sage, however, is generally non-toxic, *though it should be avoided during pregnancy*. It is extremely euphoric and so is very good as an antidepressant. In fact, it has quite an intoxicating effect and so should never be used on someone who has been drinking! It blends well with sandalwood and lavender, and has rather a sweet scent. It is safe to use for children and has a very calming effect on them, too, if mixed into a bath.
Other uses: As a general tonic and sedative; for menstrual problems, both period pains and scanty, irregular periods.

Geranium *(below)*
(Pelargonium odorantissimum/graveolens)
The sweet scent of this oil is strong but fresh rather than cloying and it blends well with a very wide range of other oils, including lavender, rose, patchouli, neroli and bergamot. It has antidepressant and sedative properties and is good for anxiety, stress and mood swings.
OTHER USES: Many skin problems, including eczema and acne; throat infections; diarrhoea; burns; as an insect repellent. Safe for children.

Jasmine *(above)*
(Jasminum officinale)
Jasmine is one of the most powerful of the antidepressant oils. It has an exquisitely sweet floral fragrance which blends with other oils such as rose, clary sage and the citrus oils. It is another expensive oil. As well as being an anti-depressant, it has aphrodisiac and sedative properties. It should be used only in moderation – both in terms of quantity in a blend (usually two or three drops are sufficient) and frequency.
OTHER USES: Coughs and catarrh; female reproductive problems, especially labour pains, to increase breast milk and for post-natal depression.

Vetivert
(Andropogen muricatus)
Vetivert is traditionally associated with men's toiletries and its woody, smoky aroma contrasts with many of the more flowery scents of the relaxing oils – making this a good one to use if you are going to give a massage to a man. Vetivert comes from a tall, scented grass and has a deeply relaxing effect. It is ideal for use in the bath or for massage, where it blends well with lavender.

Lemon *(below)*
(Citrus limon)
Lemon is a very refreshing, cleansing oil and this uplifting quality can be useful for depression and fatigue. The oil comes from the peel of the fruit and has a very distinctive citrus smell that combines well with, among others, bergamot, geranium, ginger, eucalyptus and juniper. Besides its emotionally clarifying properties, the oil is renowned, like lemon juice, for strengthening the immune system, particularly against colds, fever, flu and infections. *Lemon oil is phototoxic – do not use on the skin before exposure to sunlight.*
OTHER USES: Sinusitis; asthma; brittle nails; insect bites. It has also been suggested that it can dissolve kidney stones.

Lavender *(above)*
(Lavandula officinalis/angustifolia)
If you had to choose just one oil to take with you to a desert island that would suit every circumstance, it would almost certainly be lavender. This versatile oil derives from the flowers of the herb and it has a familiar fresh scent, often used in perfume. It is one of the safest essences to use – even for children – and one of the few that can be used directly on the skin without being blended in carrier oil. It is both antiseptic and healing, particularly on burns (where it promotes skin regeneration), bites and stings. It blends extremely well with most other oils (especially floral or citrus) and has strong sedative and calming properties, making it very effective for problems such as tension, depression and insomnia.
OTHER USES: Headaches; skin problems; high blood pressure; respiratory and digestive disorders; cystitis; sunburn. It is useful for any inflammatory condition, as a painkiller and as an antiseptic.

Rose
Rosa damascena **(damask rose)**
Rosa centifolia **(cabbage rose)**
The rose has been prized since antiquity for its healing and regenerative powers. Its scent is, of course, heady and very feminine, and it is commonly linked in aromatherapy to female problems, such as regulating menstrual periods. It is strongly antidepressant and aphrodisiac, and works well for most emotional problems with its stabilizing and uplifting qualities. It blends well with most other flower essences. It works particularly well in skin preparations and is even said to have powers of rejuvenation! It is one of the gentlest oils and its stabilizing effect works equally well on the heart and circulation as well as headaches. It is one of the most expensive oils but, as it has such a powerful aroma, a little goes a long way.
OTHER USES: Headache; eczema; hayfever; as an antiseptic. Safe for children.

Basil *(right)*
(Ocimum basilicum)
Basil is one of the most uplifting oils and works especially well with emotional problems connected with anxiety and mental fatigue. Used in the bath or simply inhaled from a tissue, it gives an instant boost – concentrating the mind and strengthening confidence. It is also quite a powerful antiseptic and is excellent for respiratory problems such as bronchitis, colds, coughs and sinusitis. It blends well with clary sage, bergamot and geranium. *It should, however, be used only in moderation and never during pregnancy.*
OTHER USES: Muscular aches and pains; rheumatism; as an insect repellant.

Sandalwood *(above)*
(Santalum album)
This warm, sweet, woody essence comes from the tropical sandalwood tree and has been known in the East for its medicinal, cosmetic and embalming properties for thousands of years. It has a calming, anti-depressant effect and is also said to have aphrodisiac properties. Many men find it more appealing than the more flowery essences. It combines well with such resonating scents as rose and neroli, and is an important constituent in many perfumes.
OTHER USES: For the respiratory system, especially sore throats and laryngitis; insomnia; diarrhoea; as a diuretic; for dry skin.

Therapeutic Starter Pack

Essential oils can be very effective in treating certain conditions. While it would be foolish to suggest they can be used exclusively to cure a whole range of medical problems, they are often able, within their limitations, to give relief to people suffering from such conditions as rheumatism and arthritis, back pain, respiratory problems and a whole range of minor ailments. This starter-pack of 11 oils does not include such delicious fragrances as those found in the relaxing starter pack. However, they can be mixed with some of them, the most important of which is lavender. The therapeutic properties of this oil are on a par with its relaxing ones. Other oils with strongly therapeutic powers include clary sage, sandalwood and lemon (pages11-13); camomile (page 18); and tea tree, fennel and marjoram (page 17).

Cypress *(above)*
(Cupressus sempervirens)
The smoky, woody aroma of cypress has a very soothing effect and so is very useful for anxiety and insomnia. It has a remarkable ability to staunch the flow of blood and is excellent for stopping nose bleeds. It is very helpful for varicose veins (though it may only prevent the worsening of the condition, as opposed to curing it), haemorrhoids and oily skin. It blends well with cedarwood, lavender, clary sage and citrus oils.
OTHER USES: Cellulite; spasmodic coughing and bronchitis; swollen joints; wounds.

Bergamot
(Citrus bergamia)
The essential oil does not come from the herb called bergamot, but from the fruit of the bergamot tree. It is extracted from the rind of the fruit, which resembles a small orange and so it has a fresh, sweet citrus smell. Its uplifting, refreshing quality gives it as much value as a relaxing oil (for depression, anxiety and stress) as a therapeutic one. It is excellent as an antiseptic, notably on a vaporizer against airborne infections. It is also very effective for skin problems such as acne, eczema and psoriasis, *but should not be used on skin before exposure to sunlight.*
OTHER USES: As an insect repellant and on insect bites; sore throats, halitosis, tonsillitis; cystitis and thrush.

Ginger *(below)*
(Zingiber officinale)
Ginger is noted for its warming qualities and so is particularly effective for respiratory problems. Used sparingly in a blend with oils such as lemon, coriander and patchouli, it has a stimulating, effect. This makes it useful for all sorts of muscular aches and pains, arthritis, rheumatism, sprains and poor circulation. *It should not be used on the skin before exposure to sunlight.*
OTHER USES: Nausea and travel sickness; constipation.

Cedarwood *(above)*

(Juniperus virginiana)

The oil from the Virginian cedar has a smell which inevitably reminds one of pencils as this is its principal product. The ancient Egyptians, however, prized the cedar of Lebanon as an ingredient for mummification and cosmetics. It is excellent for respiratory problems, such as bronchitis, catarrh and coughs. Its other principal use is in skin complaints such as eczema and dermatitis. It blends well with sandalwood, cypress, juniper, rose and patchouli. *Do not use during pregnancy.*

OTHER USES: Cystitis; dandruff, oily hair and skin; as an insect repellant.

Frankincense

(Boswellia thurifera)

The high value of frankincense in the ancient world is reflected in it being one of the three gifts offered to the baby Jesus. It has certain similarities to myrrh, one of the other gifts, but has a warmer, lighter, sweet fragrance. It is useful for rheumatism and arthritis, cystitis and menstrual problems, and as an inhalant for catarrh, laryngitis and bronchitis. Blend with lavender, sandalwood, rose, bergamot, neroli and other spices.

OTHER USES: Anxiety and stress.

It has also been prized for thousands of years as a rejuvenator for dry, mature skin and is said to stimulate cell renewal.

Myrrh *(below)*

(Commiphora myrrha/ Balsamodendron myrrha)

Myrrh shares many of the characteristics and properties of frankincense, though it has a slightly more musky, bitter smell and a more strengthening therapeutic effect. It is particularly useful for mouth ulcers and for healing cuts and wounds. Like frankincense, it is thought to be good for the complexion. It blends with other woody, spicy oils such as frankincense, sandalwood, cedarwood and ginger. *It should never be used in pregnancy.*

OTHER USES: Coughs, colds and bronchitis; stretchmarks; thrush.

Rosemary *(above)*

(Rosmarinus officinalis)

As well as being an excellent antiseptic, rosemary has a generally warming, stimulating and balancing effect on all the internal organs. It has a similar effect on the mind to that of basil – invigorating and strengthening. It is particularly useful for rheumatism, arthritis and general muscular aches and pains. It is traditionally used in many hair preparations. It combines well with other herbal oils and cedarwood. *Do not use during pregnancy.*

OTHER USES: Coughs, colds and flu.

Juniper
(Juniperus communis)
Juniper is a diuretic and very effective for urinary infections and fluid retention, especially during menstruation. It is the most powerful ingredient in the recipe on page 51 for cystitis and, in expelling uric acid from the joints, it is also useful for rheumatism, arthritis and gout. It stimulates the circulation, purifies the bloodstream and acts on the kidneys. It is also excellent for indigestion and flatulence. It blends well with lavender, cypress, rosemary and cedarwood. Use only the oil made from the berry rather than that from the wood. *It should not be used during pregnancy, nor for those with kidney disease.*

Benzoin
(Styrax benzoin)
Benzoin used to be known as gum benjamin and it is made from the gum of the tropical benzoin tree. It is one of the most familiar of incense smells. It has an overall warming effect and, when mixed with other oils and used as an inhalant, it is excellent for colds, coughs, bronchitis and flu – all conditions that respond to its warming properties. It is also beneficial for urinary infections, such as cystitis, and for skin problems, such as dermatitis. It blends well with sandalwood.
OTHER USES: For rheumatism and arthritis, as a compress; as a general sedative.

Clove *(above)*
(Syzygium aromaticum)
The spicy smell of clove is familiar from its widespread use in cooking. It has long been associated with relief from toothache, though it can also be used (one or two drops in a blend with other oils, such as rose, bergamot and lavender) as a compress for wounds, bruises and burns. There are various types of clove oil – made from the leaf, stem or bud. For home use, always use the clove bud oil as the others can cause skin irritation.
OTHER USES: Arthritis and rheumatism; as part of a steam inhalation for bronchitis; as a mosquito repellant.

Eucalyptus *(below)*
(Eucalyptus globulus)
Eucalyptus has a good deal in common with basil oil and delivers the same boost to the system, energizing and invigorating mind and body. Its distinctive aroma is well known from its use in proprietary decongestant medicines for colds. It is an extremely powerful natural antiseptic and a few drops on the pillow or a vaporizer can often ward off potential colds and infections. It can be blended with lemon, lavender, pine and cypress.
OTHER USES: Rheumatism and arthritis; cystitis (use in bath); cold sores; headaches; all respiratory disorders; against infection.

First Aid

There are a number of multi-purpose oils that make up an ideal first aid kit to deal with minor emergencies, to be used either at home or to take on holiday. As always, lavender is indispensable (see page 13) – it can be used directly on the skin and has excellent soothing, healing and antiseptic properties. It is also a stabilizing and uplifting oil on an emotional level and is good at dispelling headaches and relieving insomnia. Eucalyptus, rosemary and peppermint are also very useful in the medicine cabinet, between them treating a wide variety of ailments from colds to indigestion. Two other emergency essentials are not aromatherapy oils, but to be highly recommended nonetheless. One is arnica cream or ointment which has an outstanding ability to prevent bruising. The other is a Bach flower remedy, "Rescue Remedy", which is ideal in cases of shock and trauma.

Tea tree
(Melaleuca alternifolia)
This remarkable oil comes from an Australian tree and, while the essence is a comparative newcomer to aromatherapy, it has been used by Australian aborigines for many years. It is an extremely useful therapeutic oil and a prodigious antiseptic. It soothes and heals wounds and is useful against skin infections, mouth ulcers, cystitis, insect bites and stings, blisters and burns, spots and acne, nappy rash, and fungal infections like athlete's foot and ringworm. It fights off colds, coughs, sore throats, cold sores and flu, and eases diarrhoea. It also soothes sunburn and is an effective insect repellant. It blends well with lavender, clary sage, rosemary, marjoram and geranium.
OTHER USES: Thrush, bronchitis.

Marjoram *(right)*
(Origanum majorana)
This familiar culinary herb produces a woody aroma with a warming, comforting quality. The oil is very effective against bruising and for soothing sprains, strains, and general muscular aches and pains. It is excellent massaged into the temples to alleviate headache and migraine, and has a calming effect emotionally, making it useful against insomnia and tension. It is also renowned for alleviating period pains and PMT, constipation, flatulence and indigestion. It mixes well with other herbal oils, tea tree and eucalyptus. *It should not be used during pregnancy.*
OTHER USES: High blood pressure; colds and bronchitis; rheumatism and arthritis.

Fennel *(above)*
(Foeniculum vulgare)
Fennel is another well-known culinary herb and its essential oil is mostly noted for its calming and toning effects on the digestive system. This means it is particularly good in cases of nausea and vomiting, colic, constipation, flatulence and even hiccoughs. It is also used as a diuretic and for dissolving kidney stones. Traditionally, it is supposed to increase mothers' milk. It blends well with geranium, lavender and sandalwood. *It should not be used during pregnancy or by epileptics.*
OTHER USES: Bruising; cellulite; obesity; asthma; bronchitis.

Children's Starter Pack

A starter-pack of aromatherapy oils is particularly useful for children – few mothers want to subject babies and young children to drugs and antibiotics and their possible side-effects, if they can avoid it. Any essences to be used for children must, of course, be very gentle ones and *you should only use the ones mentioned here or on page 59.* Yet again, lavender is one of the most useful oils – it is very gentle, soothing and healing, and effective against everything from sleeplessness to nappy rash. It can be applied neat even to a child's delicate skin. Other useful oils for children include geranium, rose and clary sage (pages11-13); eucalyptus (page 16), and tea tree (page 17).

Mandarin *(above)*
(Citrus reticulata)
The very sweet citrus smell of this oil and its gentle, soothing properties make it ideal for children. It blends well with geranium and is good for hiccoughs, stomach upsets, insomnia and for calming down over-excited or tearful children as it has the dual ability of simultaneously calming and lifting the spirits.
OTHER USES: To prevent stretchmarks in pregnancy; fluid retention; obesity; for digestive and liver problems in the elderly.

Camomile
(Anthemis nobilis /Roman camomile)
(Matricaria chamomilla /German camomile)
With lavender, camomile is probably the most important essential oil for children. It is extremely gentle and calming while at the same time being antiseptic, anti-inflammatory and anti-spasmodic. This makes it ideal for a very wide range of childhood ailments from teething pain, earache, colic, vomiting and diarrhoea to convulsions, tantrums and sleeplessness. It can be used on nappy rash, burns and scalds. It is very soothing blended with lavender, rose, geranium or clary sage in the bath or as a massage oil.
OTHER USES: Acne and eczema; rheumatism and arthritis; muscular aches and pains.

Peppermint *(left)*
(Mentha piperita)
Peppermint oil has a strong, distinctive smell and is more suitable for older than for very young children. It is useful in relieving toothache (applied on a cotton bud directly to the teeth) and for nausea and travel sickness. It is good for older children's stomach aches and for colds and flu. It is an excellent antiseptic and as it has sedative qualities, can have a quite calming, soothing effect on over-excited children. It relieves itchiness of the skin so helps to soothe chickenpox symptoms. It blends well with lavender and eucalyptus.
OTHER USES: Headache and migraine; bronchitis; sinusitis; palpitations; ringworm and scabies.

OTHER OILS

Besides the oils mentioned in the starter-packs, there are many more essences available that are suitable for home use. There are still others that have ambiguous or toxic properties which make them difficult for the non-professional to use. Those listed here are safe and effective for home use unless otherwise indicated. Some act as substitutes for more common or more expensive oils, while others have curative powers over very specific ailments.

Petitgrain *(above)*
(Citrus aurantium)
This is one of the three essences to come from the orange tree, this one from the leaf. Petitgrain has a good deal in common with neroli which comes from the blossom of the tree. It has a fresh, uplifting flowery aroma and is frequently used in hair and skin care. It is also a natural deodorant.
OTHER USES: Insomnia; nervous exhaustion.

Melissa (Lemon balm) *(left)*
(Melissa officinalis)
This gentle, soothing essence balances the emotions and acts as a general tonic – on the heart, the nervous system and the menstrual cycle (where it regulates the periods and soothes menstrual pain). On an emotional level, it is antidepressant, calming and uplifting. It has similarities both to neroli and bergamot.
OTHER USES: Flatulence, nausea and vomiting; as an insect repellant.

Rosewood
Aniba rosaeodora
Though this oil is actually extracted from the tropical evergreen rosewood tree, it has the relaxing and emotional balancing qualities associated with the more expensive essence of rose and is often used as a substitute for it. It has a sweet, floral fragrance, though not the heady quality of rose, and blends well with sandalwood, bergamot and geranium. It has a calming, steadying effect and is good for insomnia, headaches, nervous tension and nausea. It also stimulates the immune system.
OTHER USES: General skin care; colds, coughs and flu.

Orange *(below)*
(Citrus sinensis)
This third of the orange oils comes from the rind of the fruit and has a soothing and uplifting quality and a sweet, fresh smell. It is a relaxing essence and is helpful in stress-related conditions and insomnia. It blends well with spicy oils such as clove or with lavender and clary sage. *Like most citrus oils, it should not be used on the skin before exposure to sunlight.*
OTHER USES: Colds, flu and bronchitis; water retention; skin care for oily skin.

Pine *(above)*
(Pinus sylvestris)
This refreshing, stimulating oil has a clean smell of pine and makes an excellent inhalant for blocked sinuses, catarrh and general congestion. It is also used for rheumatism, arthritis and muscular aches and pains where it has a quite invigorating effect. It works on an emotional level in much the same way as cypress and is good for nervous exhaustion and fatigue. Also, like cypress, it is a natural deodorant. Blend with cedarwood, rosemary and patchouli.
OTHER USES: Cystitis and urinary infections.

Camphor
(Cinnamomum camphora)
Camphor oil is extracted from the wood of this tropical evergreen tree. As an essential oil, when used by a trained aromatherapist, it can have a very marked effect. However, as it can be a strong stimulant to the heart, it is best left to the professional therapists and only for severe ailments. In this context, however, it has various uses – respiratory ailments, for both diarrhoea and constipation and as a tonic for the heart, the circulation of the blood and the respiratory system.

Black pepper *(below)*
(Piper nigrum)
Essence of black pepper has a warm, spicy scent and a stimulating, warming action both physically and emotionally. It is a good remedy for colds, flu and fever. It also acts on the digestive system, on colic, constipation, diarrhoea, flatulence and loss of appetite. It stimulates the circulation and is helpful before and after exercise as it warms up the muscles and is good for sprains. It should only be used very moderately, mixed with other essences such as frankincense, sandalwood, lavender and rosemary.
OTHER USES: Rheumatism and arthritis; anaemia; haemorrhoids.

Tagetes *(above)*
(Tagetes minuta)
Although this oil comes from a plant closely related to French and African marigolds, it is often wrongly confused with the true marigold, the oil from which is rarely available. It is an excellent air freshener and insect repellant. Inhaled in this way, it promotes mental stimulation. It blends well with clary sage, lavender and bergamot, *but it should be used extremely sparingly on the skin.*
OTHER USES: Bunions, callouses and corns.

Patchouli
(Pogostemon patchouli)
The strong sensual odour of patchouli will forever be associated with the hippy 1960s! It is renowned as an antidepressant and aphrodisiac and is one of the few oils to improve with age. It is useful on cracked or chapped skin and in cases of acne, athlete's foot and eczema. It blends well with lavender, sandalwood, myrrh, neroli and clary sage.
OTHER USES: For oily skin and hair; for sharpening and focusing the mind.

Cardamon *(below)*
(Elettaria cardamomum)
Although this is a warming, sweet, slightly gingery essence, it shares many properties with peppermint. They combine well together and are excellent for nausea and heartburn. It is good for use in the bath and has an uplifting, calming – and, some say, aphrodisiac – effect on the emotions.
OTHER USES: As a general tonic, especially for those with nervous problems.

Hyssop *(above)*
(Hyssopus officinalis)
The essential oil that comes from the hyssop herb has a wide variety of uses. However it should not be used by people who suffer from epilepsy or during pregnancy and, as it does seem to have a somewhat toxic effect, it is best left to the use of a professional aromatherapist. Having said this, it is an excellent tonic when used properly – especially for people convalescing after a long illness.
OTHER USES: For bronchitis, asthma and catarrh, on bruises and wounds.

Citronella
(Cymbopogon nardus)
This powerful lemon-scented oil comes from a grass found in Sri Lanka. It is often used on a vaporizer to scent a room or to repel insects. It is used in skin care for oily skin and as a deodorant. It has a clear, uplifting quality and so is good for nervous exhaustion, headaches and migraine. Use only in small quantities and blend with geranium, bergamot, cedarwood and pine.
OTHER USES: As an antiseptic; for minor infections.

Grapefruit *(below)*
(Citrus paradisi)
This uplifting, refreshing oil has much in common with other citrus essences and it blends well with these, herbal and spicy oils. It is a good toner for oily hair and skin and it also lifts the spirits making it effective against depression, exhaustion and nervous stress. It makes a good oil for an early morning bath before a busy day. However, once bought, use it soon as it goes off more quickly than most oils.
OTHER USES: Cellulite and water retention; colds and flu.

BASIC TECHNIQUES

Essential oils work on the body in two principal ways: absorption through the skin and inhalation through the olfactory system (see page 8). A wide variety of methods of using the oils has therefore evolved, from steam inhalations to massage. Some methods are best suited to particular conditions; for instance, a steam inhalation with eucalyptus oil is ideal for congestion caused by a cold. Pressure of time and circumstances are other considerations – a massage may be impossible during the working day, but breathing in basil oil from a tissue can give your concentration and mental energy an instant boost.

While a full body massage is a real treat and the ultimate in relaxation, you can use spot do-it-yourself massage for areas of tension.

WARNING

As a general rule, essential oils are applied to the skin only when diluted in a carrier oil. There are a few cases, however, where neat oil is used – for instance, lavender on burns, cuts and insect stings. Most oils should not be used in this way and, as the results can be quite painful, don't be tempted to experiment!

MASSAGE

This is probably the best known method of using aromatherapy oils. The effect of a good massage is wonderful, as the oils penetrate through the olfactory system as well as the skin and there are the important benefits of the massage itself. The oils are always blended in a carrier oil (see page 24) and the mixture will depend upon any particular condition that is being addressed as well as personal preference.

A full body massage is demonstrated on pages 26-39 and there are individual self-help massage techniques given in the Specific Applications section (pages 40-61).

Compresses

Compresses have two main uses: to bring down swellings and sprains, and to soothe headaches. Use a clean piece of cotton fabric (a handkerchief or a towel, depending on the area to be covered). Add the essential oil to the water (1–8 drops depending on how large the compress is) and mix well. Soak the fabric, squeeze it out and place over the affected area. Use warm water for muscular aches, ice-cold water for headaches and sprains.

As the compress cools down or heats up, re-soak and re-apply. The longer you leave the compress on, the better, preferably at least an hour.

Baths

Some oil in the bath before bedtime if you suffer from insomnia can give a good night's rest (lavender is particularly good). Baths are also useful for conditions such as rheumatism and arthritis where there is painful swelling making massage inappropriate. Add 5–10 drops of oil to the water when you have filled the bath. It should not be too hot as this would make the oil evaporate. Swish the water to mix in the oil before you get in. Sitz or hip baths (or a plastic bowl) are useful for vaginal disorders and genito-urinary infections.

Steam Inhalations

Pour boiling water into a bowl, add 10 drops of the appropriate oil and breathe in deeply, covering your head and the bowl with a towel. Stay for about 10 minutes. This is very good for sinus, throat and chest infections but *this method is not to be used if you have asthma.*

Occasionally, the essential oils may be taken internally in hot water, with a teaspoonful of honey added.

On Pillows and Tissues

This is perhaps the simplest use of essential oils but, nonetheless, very effective. A drop of lavender or rose oil on the pillow at night gives a deep, restful sleep. A drop of peppermint oil on a tissue can relieve a headache, while oils such as jasmine and clary sage inhaled from a tissue can give a boost to low spirits.

A few drops of oil on a burner or light bulb ring will scent an entire room.

Honey Water

In the rare cases where internal use is recommended, honey water is preferable to plain. Put a teaspoonful of honey in a cup of hot water and stir until dissolved. Then add a drop of the appropriate oil – *but only those specifically suggested in this book.* Use honey water, too, as a base for mouthwashes and gargles.

A drop of rose or lavender oil on your pillow will ensure a good night's sleep.

Vaporization

You can buy special aromatherapy oil burners or light bulb rings to which you add a few drops of essential oil – your choice of oil depends on whether you require anti-bacterial properties (rosemary and eucalyptus are ideal) or you just want to give a pleasant scent to a room. You can also put a few drops of oil directly on to a radiator or in a bowl of warm water to achieve the same effect.

Using the Oils

Essential oils are extremely volatile – they will evaporate rapidly or deteriorate if kept in the wrong conditions. Only buy oils that are sold in airtight, dark glass bottles (never plastic). Do not expose them unstoppered to the air or to sunlight and keep them in a cool, dry place, preferably a refrigerator (though never a freezer!).

Carrier Oils

As a general rule, aromatherapy oils must be diluted in a carrier oil before they can be applied to the skin. Various types of oil can be used and any cold-pressed vegetable oil will make a good base. One consideration is the smell – olive oil, for instance, has quite an overpowering smell. Almond, grapeseed, peach or apricot kernel oils are vitamin rich and easily absorbed. Olive and wheatgerm oils are usually used with another lighter carrier oil and are particularly good for dry and mature skin, and for a massage oil to be used on the face. Coconut oil blends well with sweet floral essences. Calendula oil is excellent for problem skin.

If you want to make up a quantity of massage oil for future use, bear in mind that both vegetable and essential oils oxidize and go rancid. Keeping them, once mixed, in dark glass airtight bottles is essential. Wheatgerm oil prevents oxidization, so always use a little of this (10% or more) as part of your carrier oil.

Dark glass bottles in various sizes for storing your blended oils are usually available from chemists.

Recommended Dilutions

FOR USE ON THE BODY	FOR USE ON CHILDREN
25 drops of essential oil in *50ml (2 fl oz) carrier oil*	*10 drops of essential oil* in *50ml (2 fl oz) carrier oil*
FOR USE ON THE FACE	**FOR USE ON BABIES**
12 drops of essential oil in *50ml (2 fl oz) carrier oil*	*5 drops of essential oil* in *50ml (2 fl oz) carrier oil*

Essential oils are always diluted in carrier oils (see the table above). Peach, apricot, grapeseed, almond, coconut, calendula, olive and wheatgerm are all recommended.

BLENDING ESSENTIAL OILS

Blending essential oils is often made – rather unnecessarily – into something of a mystery. It is, in fact, a combination of common sense and personal preference. Start by measuring the correct amount of carrier oil into a dark glass bottle. If you are following one of the recipes in this book, measure in the number of drops given for each essence, stopper, shake the bottle well and, if you are not going to use it all immediately, label it.

If, however, you decide to experiment with blending, follow the simple maxim: you can add but you cannot take away. So add drops very gradually, mix and see if you feel that the blend is going to be what you want. Three (or occasionally four) should be the maximum number of essences used in any mixture. If you use more than this, the overall aroma can become muddied.

Interestingly, it is very common that the oils you like the smell of are the very ones you need therapeutically – so this is one time when you can certainly be led by your nose.

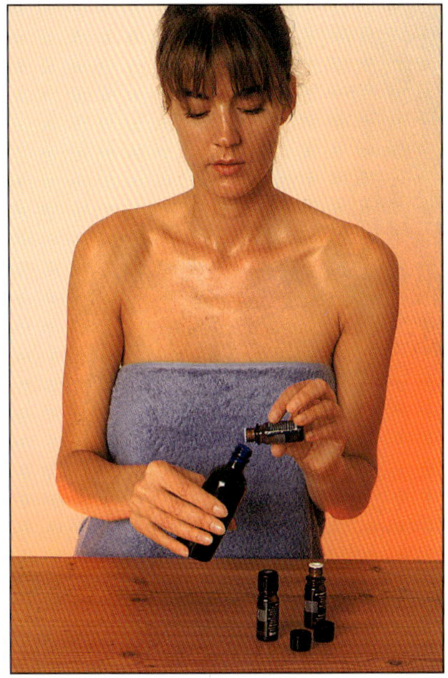

Aromatherapy oils should always be kept in dark glass bottles to protect them from the light. Put the carrier oil in first and add essential oils gradually until you achieve a scent you like.

PERFUME NOTES

In perfumery, oils are divided into groups of *top notes* (highly volatile, such as the citrus oils); *middle notes* (less volatile, such as clary sage and neroli); and *bass notes* (the longest lasting which give stability to the blend such as sandalwood). A classic blend using this method would take one from each of the groups of notes to give a balanced effect. It is not necessary, however, to follow this pattern and, indeed, there are many arguments about in which groups the various oils belong! Another approach to blending is to stick to a family of essences – for instance, using oils that all come from herbs or all from citrus fruits. In fact, there are few hard and fast rules when it comes to blending and you will find, with familiarity, you will start instinctively to put particular oils together.

TOP NOTES
– highly volatile
EXAMPLES INCLUDE: Citrus oils, such as grapefruit, lemon and orange

MIDDLE NOTES
– less volatile
EXAMPLES INCLUDE: Clary sage and neroli

BOTTOM NOTES
– most stable
EXAMPLES INCLUDE: Sandalwood

Massage Basics

Massage is one of the most ancient healing arts. It is also an instinctive response to pain – a mother will automatically "rub it better" if her child falls over. In aromatherapy terms, massage is used to help the skin to absorb the oils, as well as to encourage the body to relax. Besides relaxing tense muscles, massage can help to eliminate toxins via the skin, stimulate the circulation and, most importantly, ease mental and emotional tensions.

As the overall aim of aromatherapy massage is relaxation, the basic strokes used are gentle. The more vigorous of the strokes used in conventional Swedish massage are inappropriate. There are various methods of self-massage mentioned in the Specific Applications section of this book (pages 40-61). Here, though, the focus is on how to do a full massage. Obviously, for this, you will need a partner who will reciprocate in massaging you, too, and in this way, you will both benefit from this most luxurious and relaxing of treatments.

It is important to trust your instincts when giving a massage. Rely on your sense of touch. You will feel knotted-up muscles that need to be released and these areas may require more concentrated work. However, go gently. If you go too deeply or vigorously into an already tense muscle, it may react by going into a spasm of greater tension. Always ask if the pressure is too strong or not strong enough. Gradually, as you become more familiar with and confident of your sense of touch, you will find your hands seeming to know instinctively exactly what is needed.

Cold muscles do not relax, so it is important to keep those parts of the body that are not being worked on covered up with towels. As a rough guide, one towel is needed to lie on and at least two more to use as covers. Always work in a warm room. Ideally, you should use a massage table, but it is unlikely you will have access to one of these. You can use the floor (if you don't have a bad back – bending over can put a strain on it) or a bed.

CONTRA-INDICATIONS

There are a number of conditions when you should NOT give a massage:

Pain or inflammation of any kind is a warning sign and you should not give a massage over these areas – for instance:

- Joints swollen by rheumatism or arthritis.
- Broken, infectious or septic skin or recent scar tissue must be avoided.
- If there is any unusual lump or bump, do not touch it.
- Varicose veins should never be massaged.
- Do not massage anyone with a heart condition.

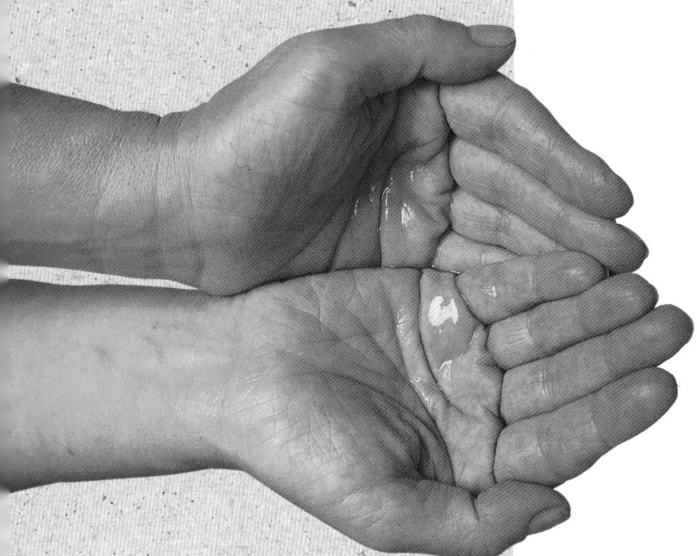

Always take time to warm the oil in your hands before the massage – the last thing your partner wants is the shock of cold oil!

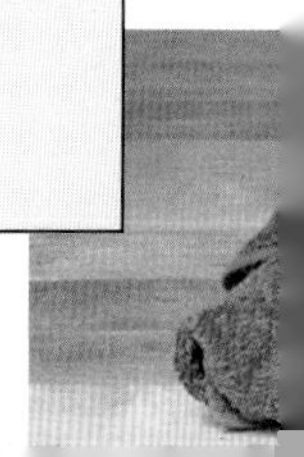

PREPARATION FOR MASSAGE

When you give a massage, you need to concentrate on it fully. So make sure you are not going to be disturbed. Choose a time – allowing yourself at least an hour and a half – when you are not going to have visitors and switch on the answering machine or unplug the phone.

The room should be warmer than you would usually have it and the lighting should be subdued. Wear loose, comfortable clothes that you can move freely in and no jewellery. You can either work in silence or play soothing music very quietly in the background.

It is best to be completely naked when being massaged – the areas not being worked on should be covered up with towels. If you are giving the massage, settle your partner under the towels and take a moment to concentrate your energies. For the next hour or so, try to leave everything else behind and live just through your sense of touch. Don't talk to your partner – unless it is to ask about the massage itself – and let any communication take place on the level of touch.

Let your whole body move in rhythm with the strokes – it is much easier than merely using the strength in your arms. Finally, always warm the oil in the palms of your hands before you apply it – applied cold, it would be a shock to your partner.

AFTER THE MASSAGE

Give your partner time to resurface – don't suddenly turn up the lights or make a noise. Wash your hands and arms in cold water to eliminate any negativity picked up from your partner during the massage. The oils will continue to work after the massage itself has finished, so don't be tempted to rush to the shower to wash it all off. The best time to receive a massage is in the evening so you can go to bed and let the oils work on your skin through the night.

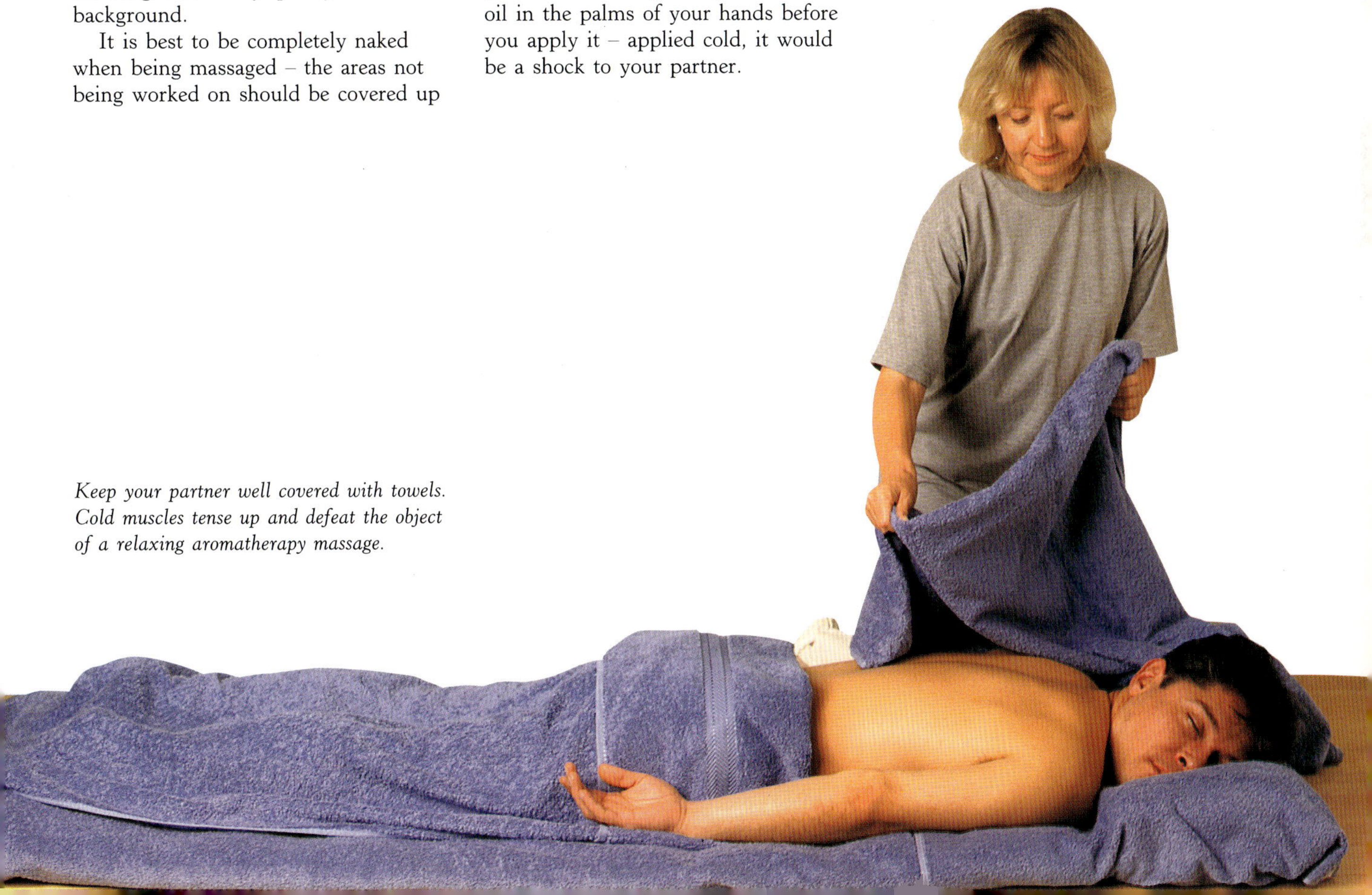

Keep your partner well covered with towels. Cold muscles tense up and defeat the object of a relaxing aromatherapy massage.

The Basic Massage Strokes

Aromatherapy massage has the ultimate aim of relaxation – so there is little of the vigorous hacking used in conventional massage – though it does have a small part to play and the technique is demonstrated here.

Although this full body massage follows a set pattern of strokes, it is important to remember that instinct and intuition have a vital part to play. If a particular stroke has a marked effect, you will no doubt want to repeat it. Conversely, if anything hurts, stop. Allow your hands to feel their own way and be your guide. The strokes mentioned here are only the basics. Once you have mastered them, you can find out more from a good massage book or simply by trying things out yourself.

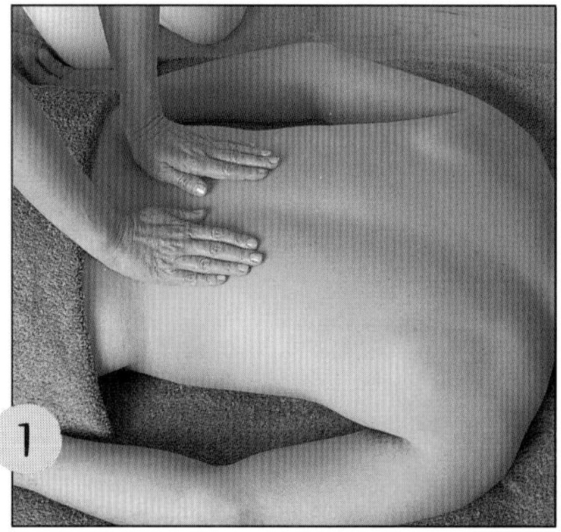

1

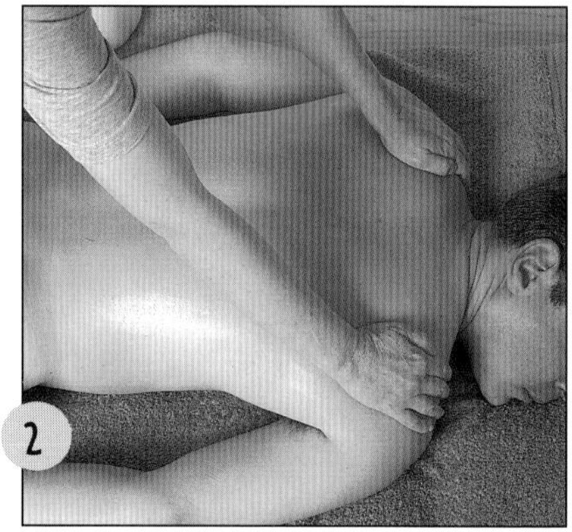

2

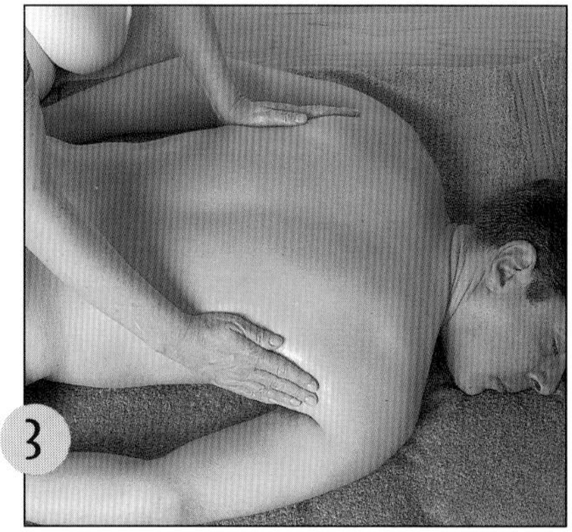

3

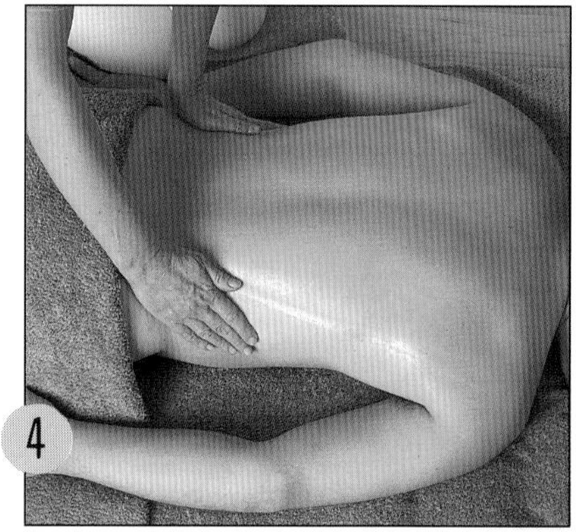

4

Effleurage

Effleurage is a long, slow rhythmic movement sometimes described as stroking and it is the most important of the techniques used in aromatherapy massage. It is done with the flat of the hands, with the fingers closed together and pointing upwards, as far as that is possible as you move.

There should be a firm, even pressure as the hands move towards the heart, and a lighter, more gliding touch on their return. Effleurage is used at the beginning and end of each stage of the massage.

At the start, it spreads oil over the body and establishes non-verbal contact with your partner. At the end, it is a signal that you have finished working on that area. From this point onwards, each repetition of the movement becomes lighter and lighter with every stroke, ending with a feather-like touch.

When massaging the back, in particular, it is a good idea to end the effleurage with the stroke known as feather stroke (see page 35).

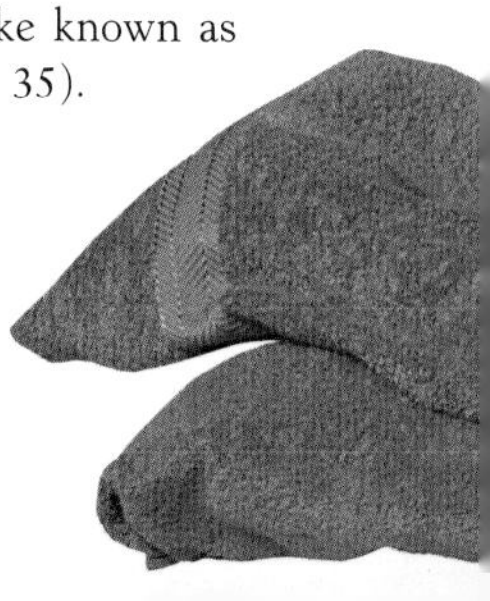

PETRISSAGE

Petrissage uses the fingers or thumbs to squeeze soft tissue against the bone immediately beneath it. It helps to eliminate accumulated toxins.

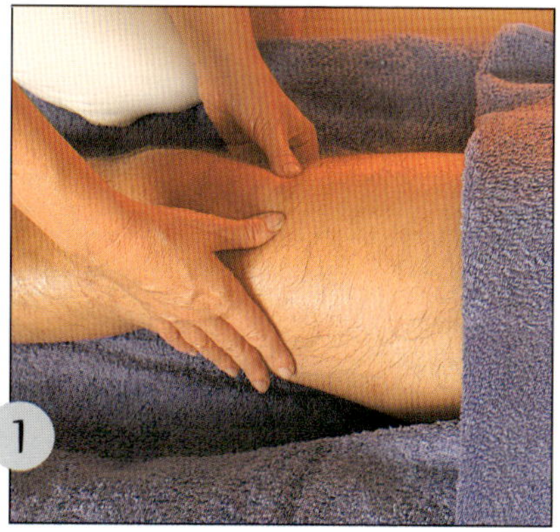

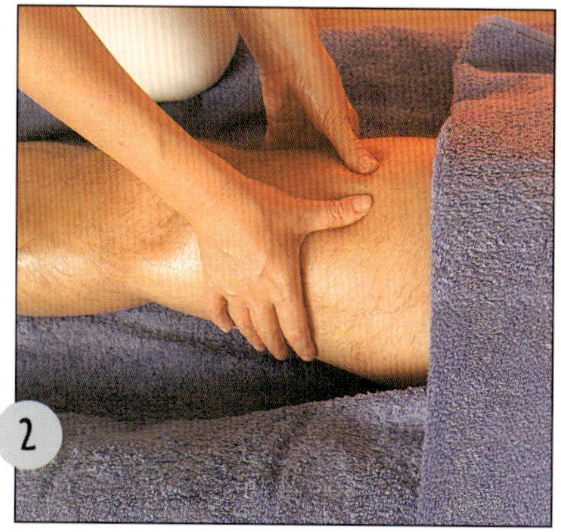

KNEADING

Kneading – the movement is just like kneading bread – is applied to soft tissue that has no bone immediately beneath it. You pick up the flesh and roll it away from the bone with a squeezing action. It relaxes tense muscles, stimulates the circulation and eliminates toxins.

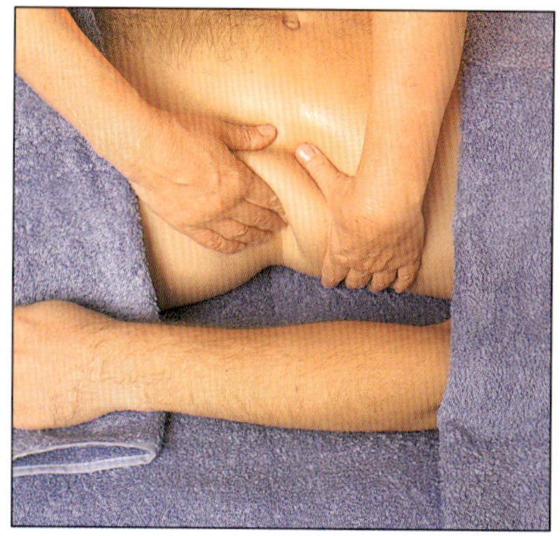

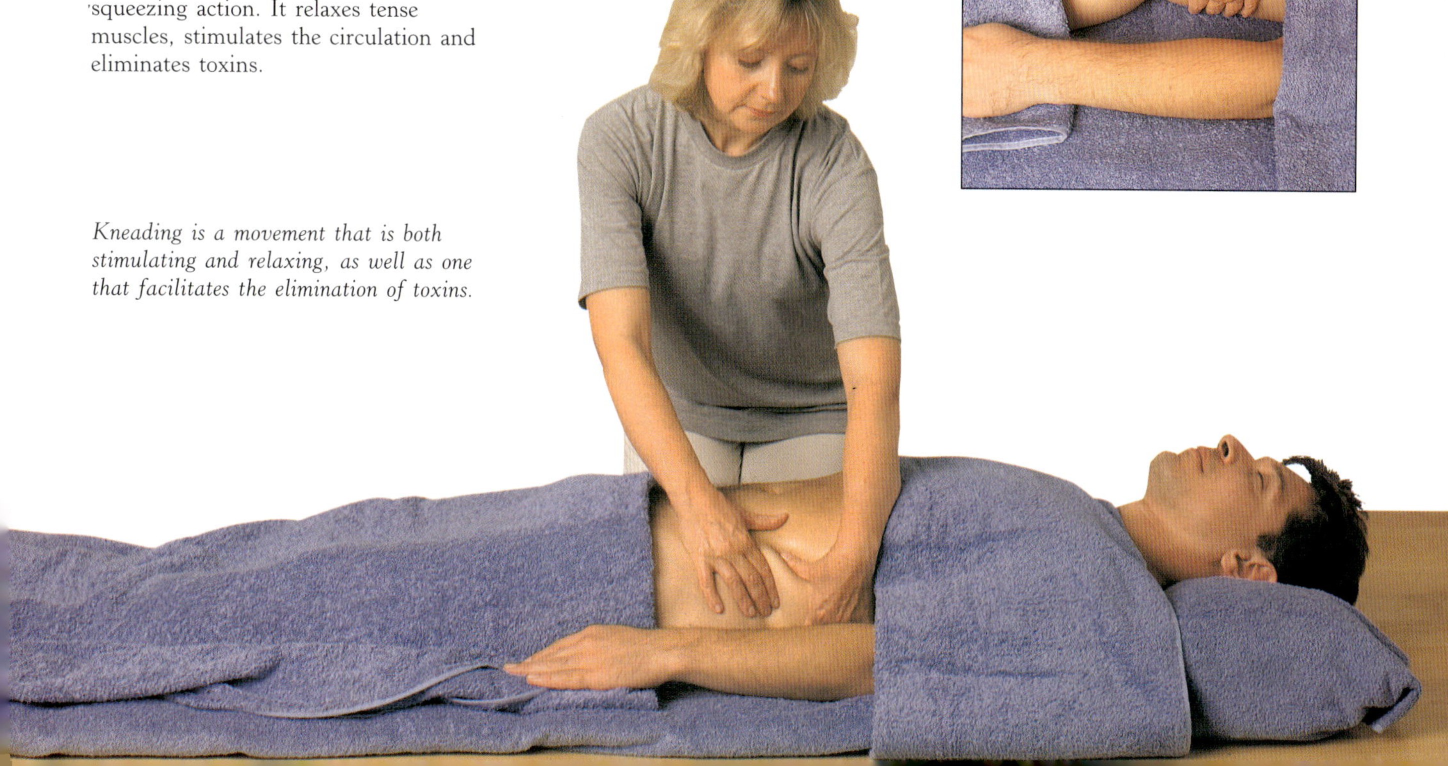

Kneading is a movement that is both stimulating and relaxing, as well as one that facilitates the elimination of toxins.

CUPPING

This is another quick movement. The hands form the shape of a cup and make a vacuum where they meet the skin. The resulting sound is like a horse trotting. Quick, alternating strokes make this an excellent toner for the circulation.

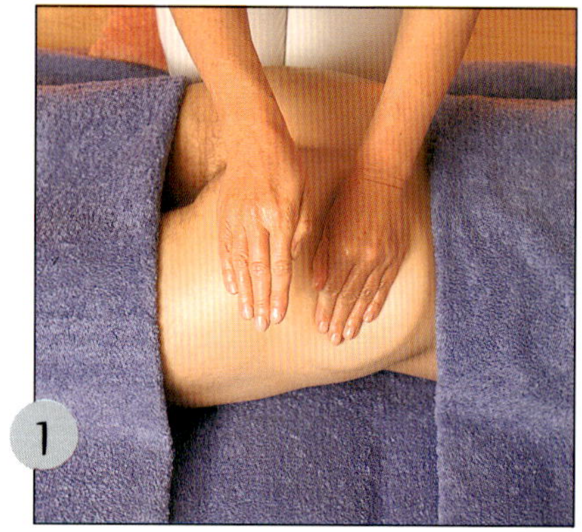

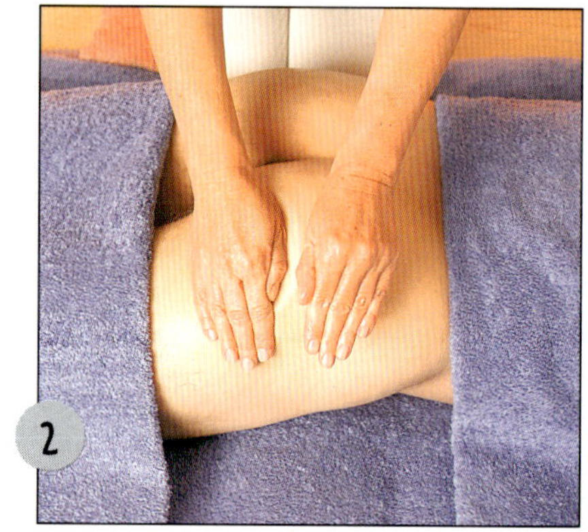

HACKING

This is a stimulating movement and only to be used very lightly and gently in aromatherapy massage. It is done using the outside edge of the little fingers, alternating in a chopping movement on areas like the calves, thighs and buttocks. Keep the hands very loose or it will be too sharp an action. This stroke is not used if the massage is aiming to induce deep relaxation.

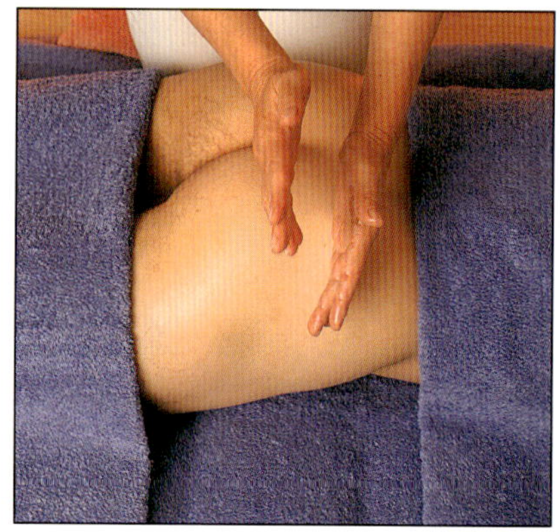

Hacking is a relatively strong movement for aromatherapy massage and only used on less sensitive areas like the calves, thighs and buttocks.

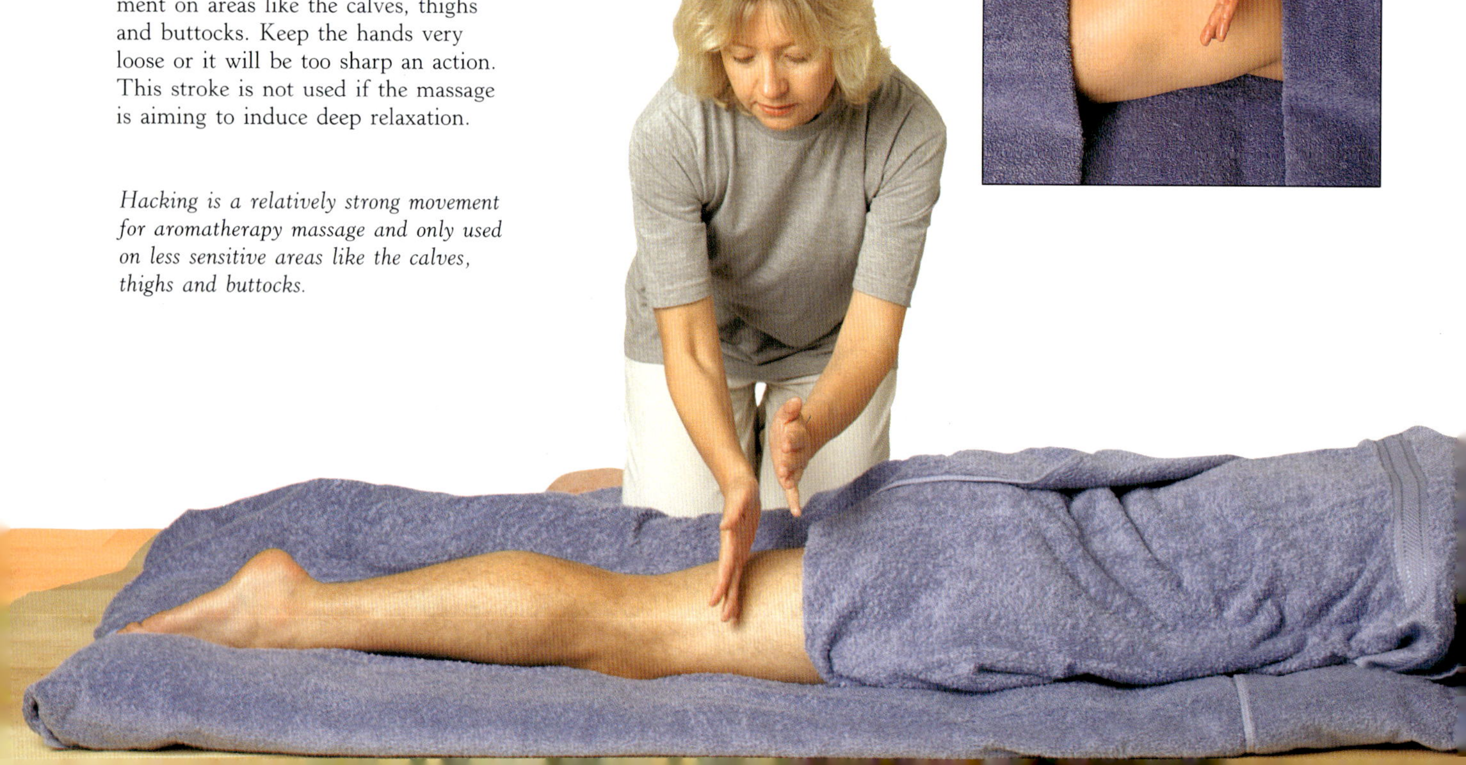

Full Body Massage

Start the massage with your partner lying face downwards. Make sure he or she is warm and comfortable and covered completely with two towels, one across the top of the body and the other over the buttocks and legs. Begin by asking your partner to take some slow, deep breaths as this will help promote relaxation. It is a good idea to do this deep breathing together as it will relax you, too, and make you feel centred.

Before you begin, make sure you are not going to be disturbed. Take the phone off the hook or switch on the answer machine.

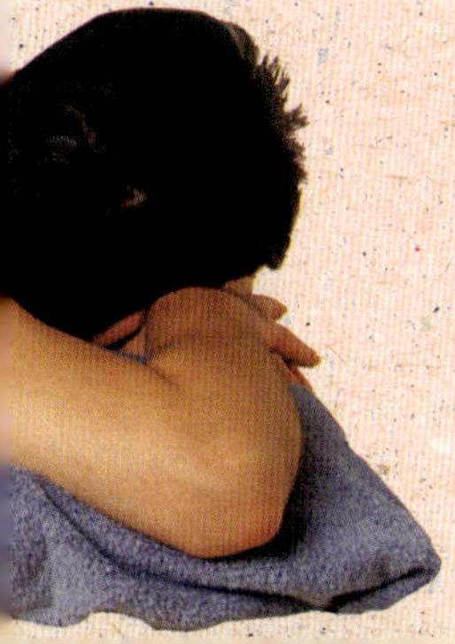

Legs

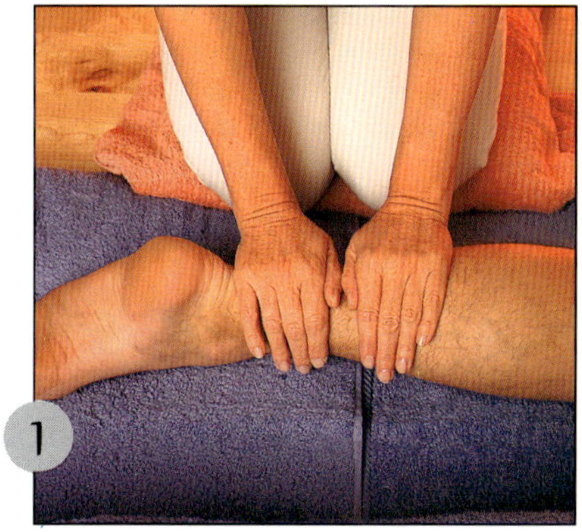

1

Uncover the right leg.

Warm some massage oil in the palms of your hands and place them flat next to each other at the bottom of the leg, near the ankle.

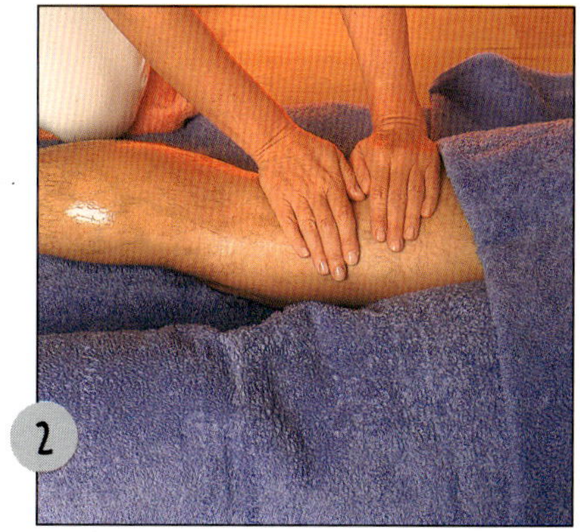

2

Gently but firmly effleurage up the centre of the leg, keeping the hands close together and the fingers closed.

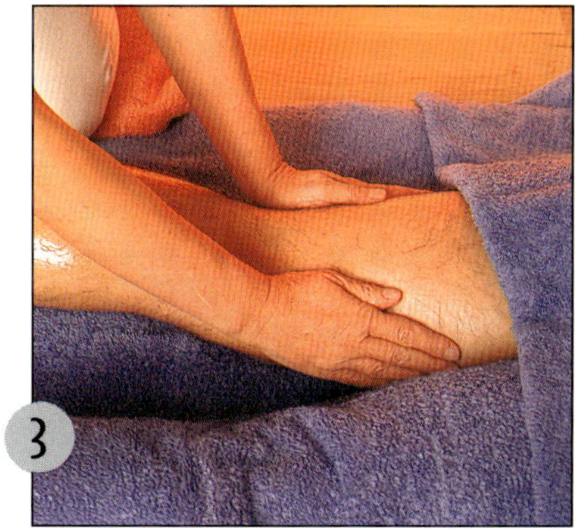

3

At the top of the leg, turn the hands so the fingers are facing upwards and move them to the outside of the thigh.

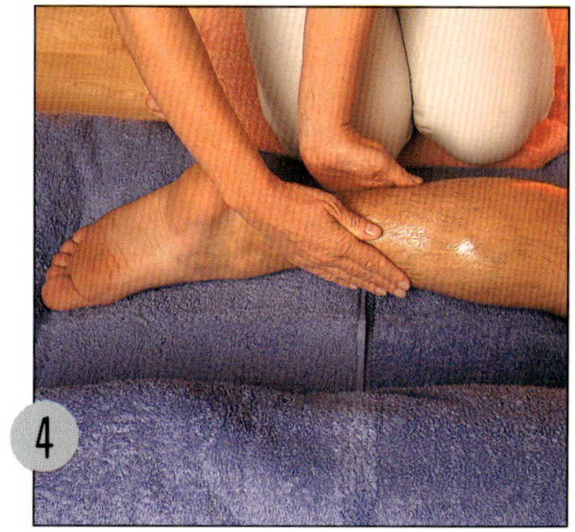

4

In a long, even sweep, bring the hands down the outer sides of the leg to the ankle. In a seamless movement, turn them so they are ready to go up the leg again. Repeat several times.

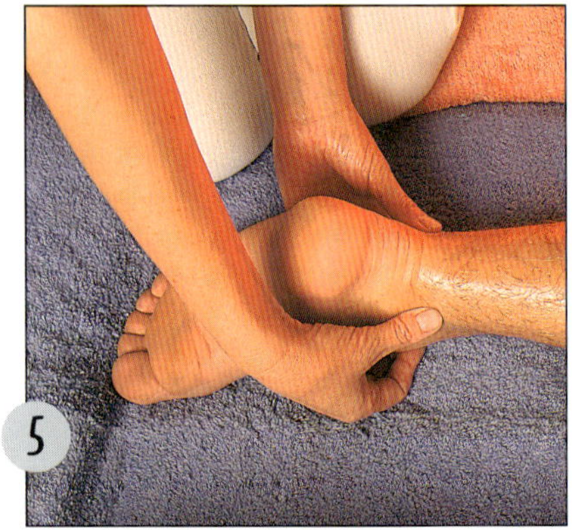

Petrissage to either side of the ankle, around the ankle bone. Do not press on the bone itself.

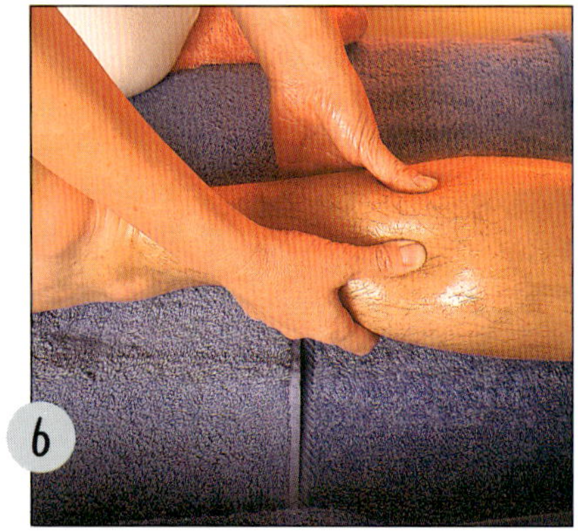

Continue the movement all the way up the centre of the leg. Be sensitive – petrissage may be too deep for some areas, particularly the back of the knee.

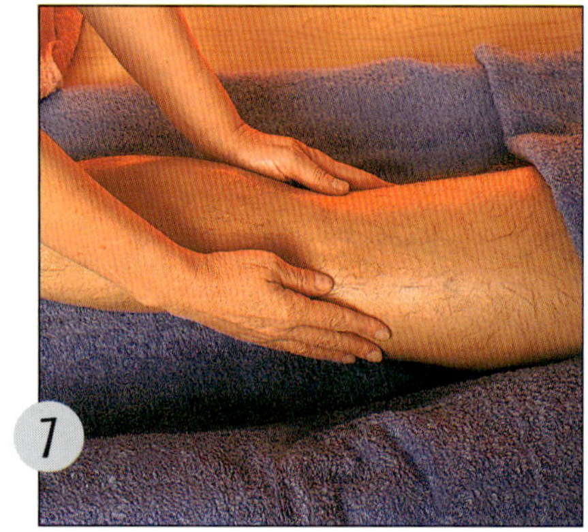

At the top of the thigh, take the hands to the outside of the leg and bring them back down to the ankle in one long sweeping movement. Repeat this several times.

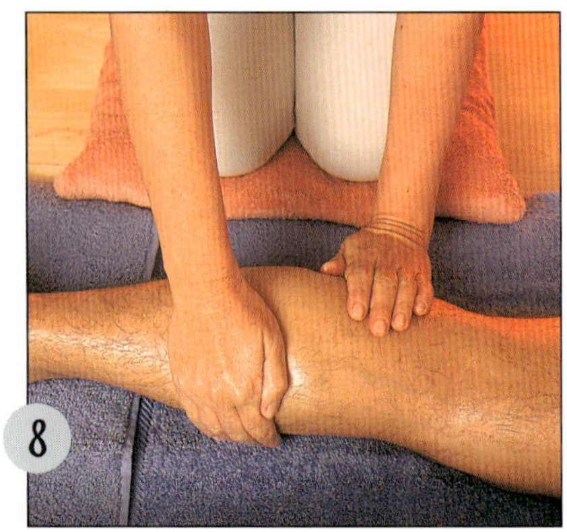

This movement – alternate effleurage – is quite vigorous and stimulating. Start at the ankle, with the hands together and then take them in opposite directions, alternating as you go.

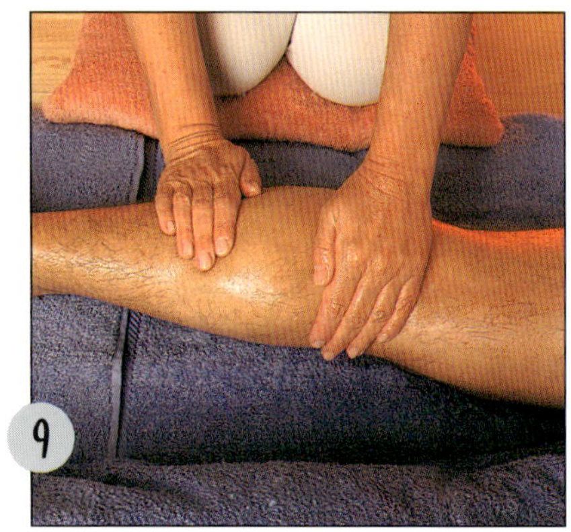

Alternate effleurage from the ankle to the top of the thigh, using the gentler stroking movement down the outer leg, as before, to return to the ankle. Repeat several times.

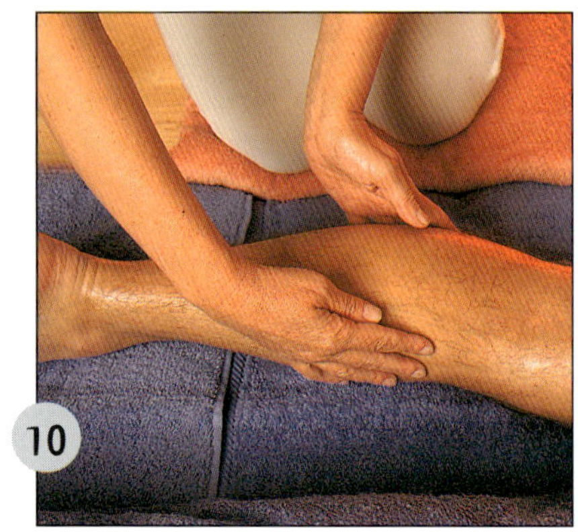

Effleurage, as at the beginning, several times, getting lighter each time. Cover the leg and repeat on the left leg.

BUTTOCKS

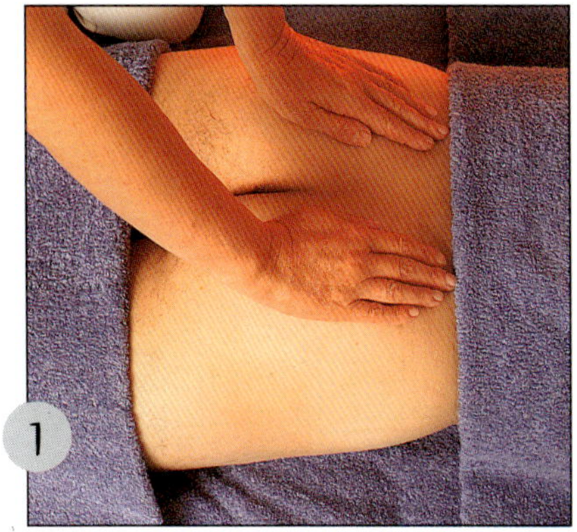

Put some more oil in your palms and warm it. Uncover the buttocks and lay one hand on each cheek.

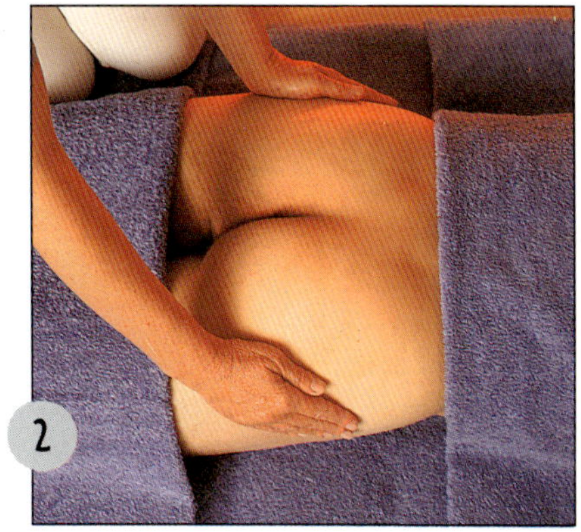

Effleurage with firm circular movements, spreading the oil over the whole area as you go.

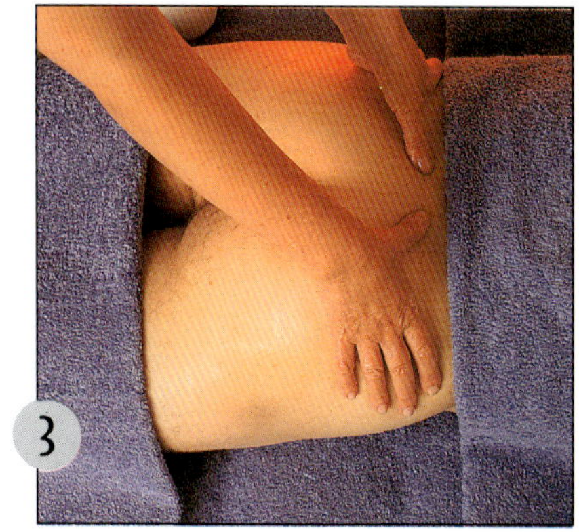

Petrissage both cheeks, starting at the spine and working outwards towards the sides with a deep pressure.

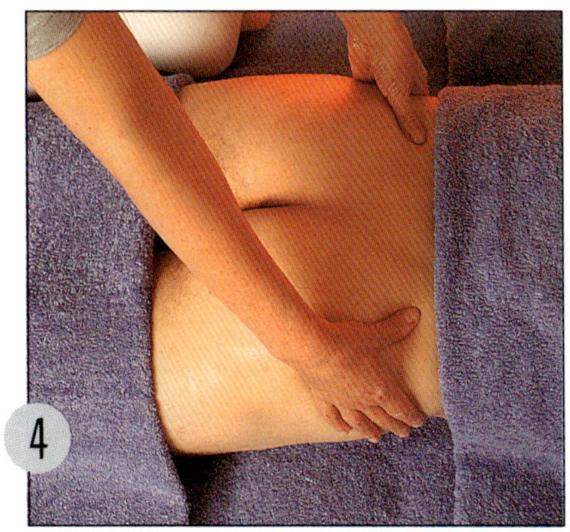

Work across the whole surface, moving down an inch each time until you reach the base of the spine. Always remember to start about an inch out from the spine – never work on the spine itself.

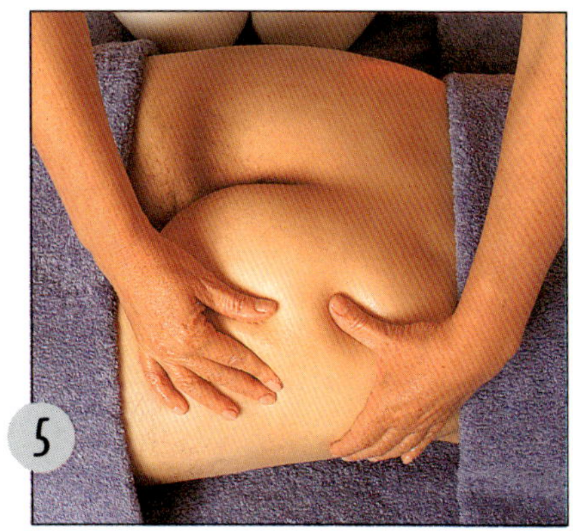

From one side of the body knead the opposite cheek. Then change sides and knead the other side.

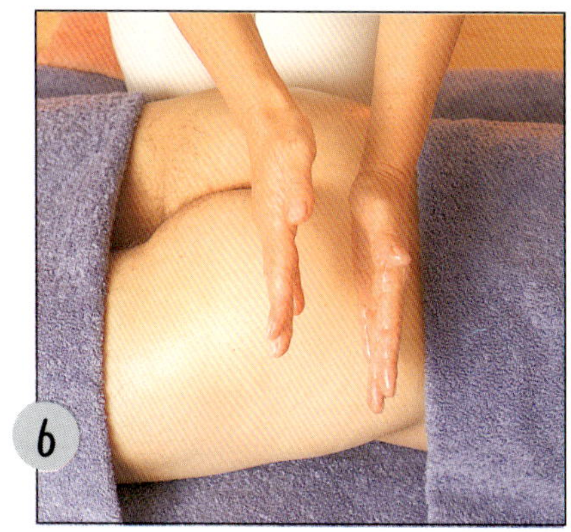

Hack and cup (see page 30) the whole cheek, then effleurage. Swap sides and repeat. Effleurage as at the start, with lighter and lighter pressure. Cover the buttocks and uncover the back.

Back

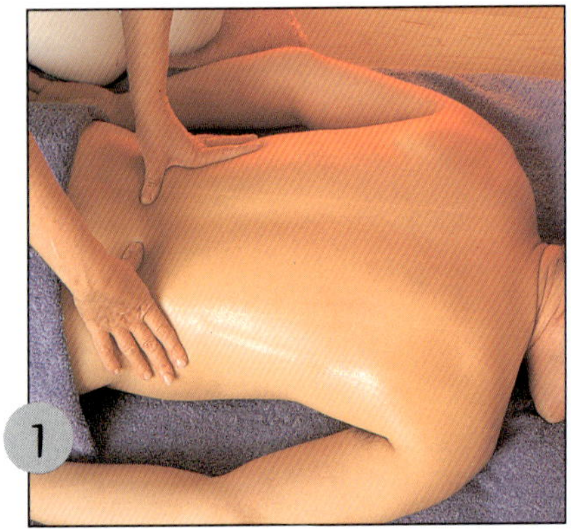

Place your hands at the base of the spine and effleurage up to the neck, gliding out over the shoulders and returning down the sides (see page 28). Repeat several times. Move the hands back to the base of the spine.

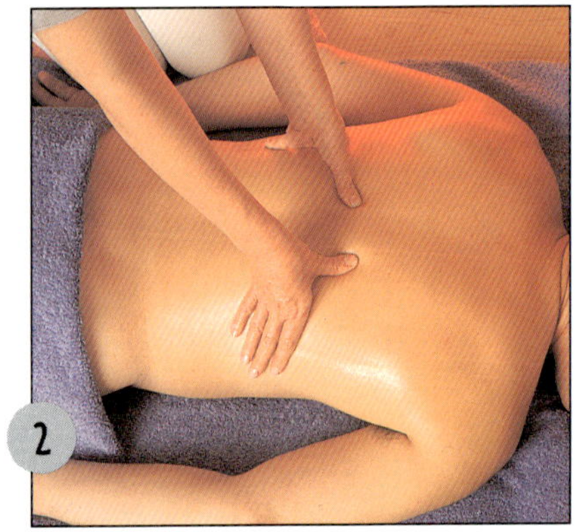

With a circular movement of the thumbs, petrissage upwards from the base of the spine to the neck, working next to the spine, not on it. Repeat several times. *Never massage the spine itself – always work at either side of it.*

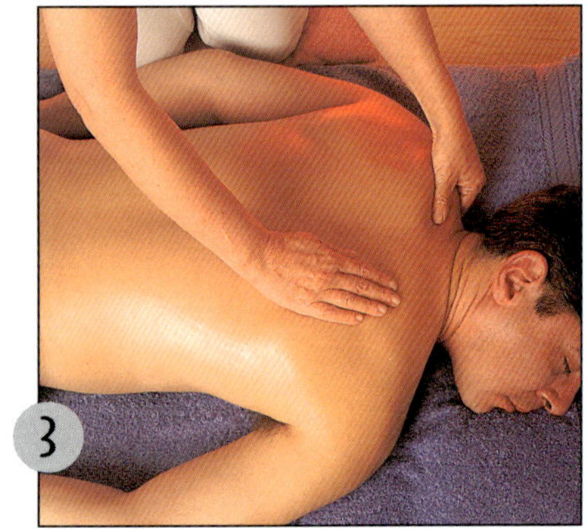

Knead the neck muscles – try to be sensitive to how your partner feels, as these muscles can often be very tense.

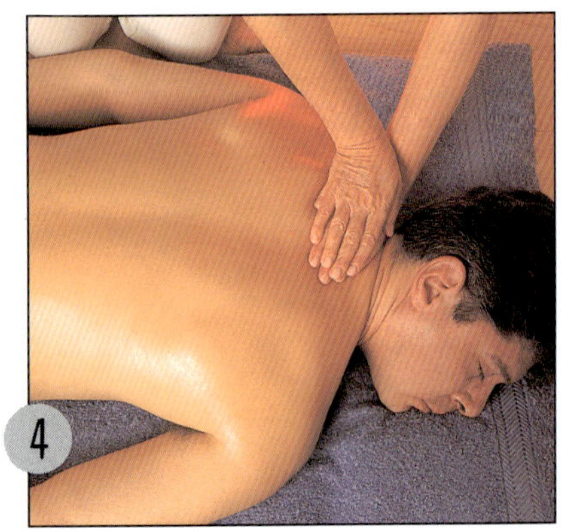

Place one hand on top of the other at the neck. This movement describes a figure of eight and you can use the weight of your body to iron out the tension.

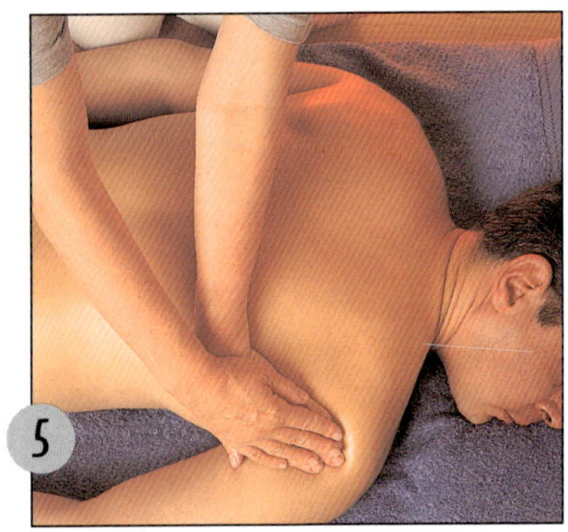

The hands move diagonally across the back to go around the opposite shoulder blade, returning to the centre and going round the first shoulder. Repeat several times.

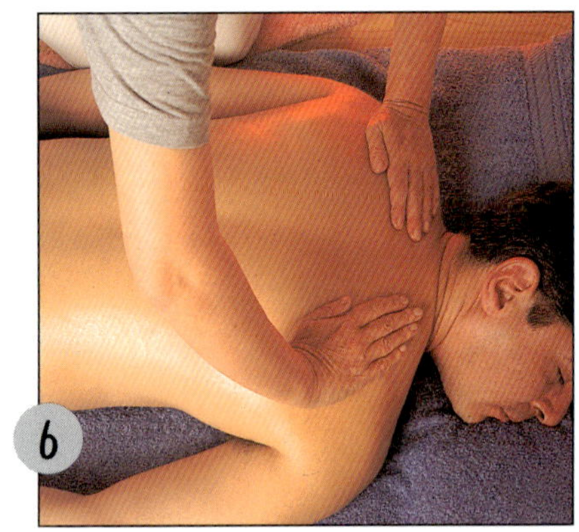

Separate the hands and do figure-of-eight movements over the whole surface of the back.

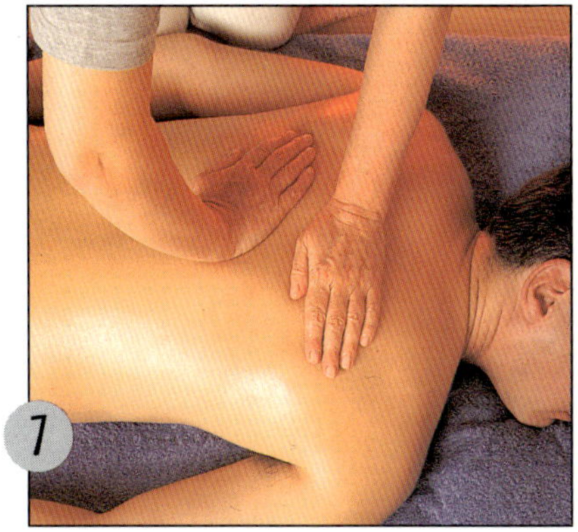

Continue this movement, travelling up and down the back, covering the whole area. Again, use your body weight in the movement.

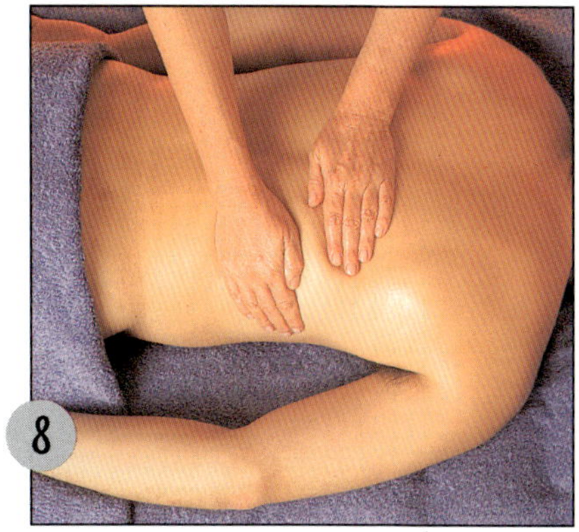

Alternate effleurage the sides of the back, starting just beneath the armpit and working down towards the waist. Change sides and repeat.

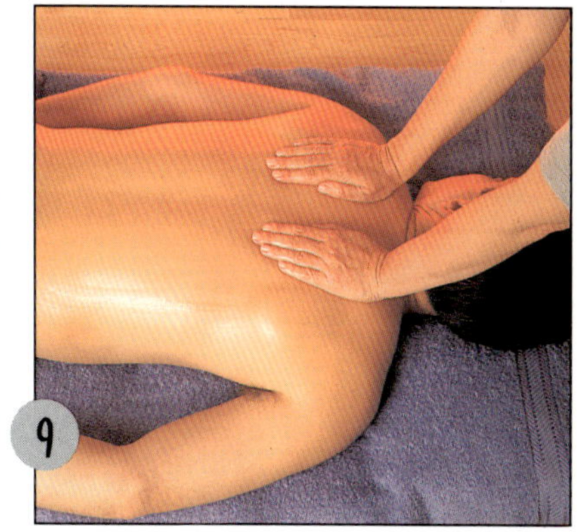

Now move around to your partner's head and effleurage down either side of the spine, again using your body weight to help release tense muscles.

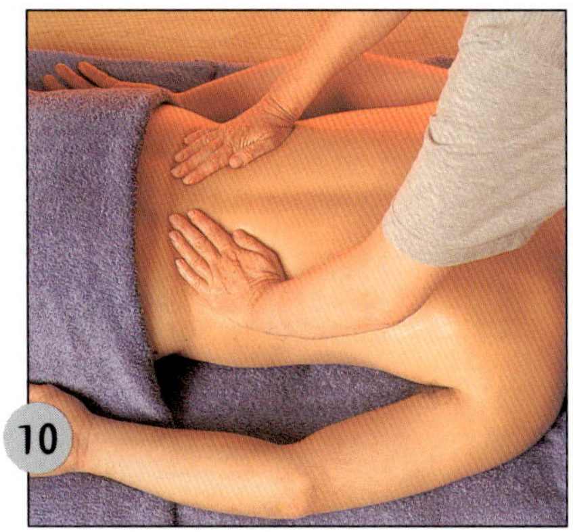

Move the hands out over the top of the buttocks and back up the sides.

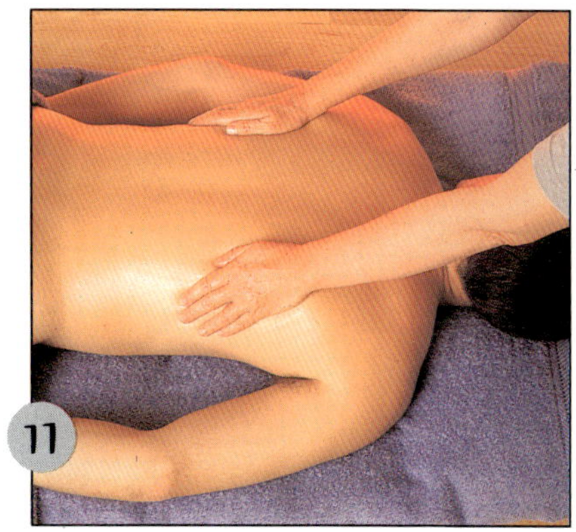

Repeat the effleurage movement several times, gradually making the pressure lighter with each repetition.

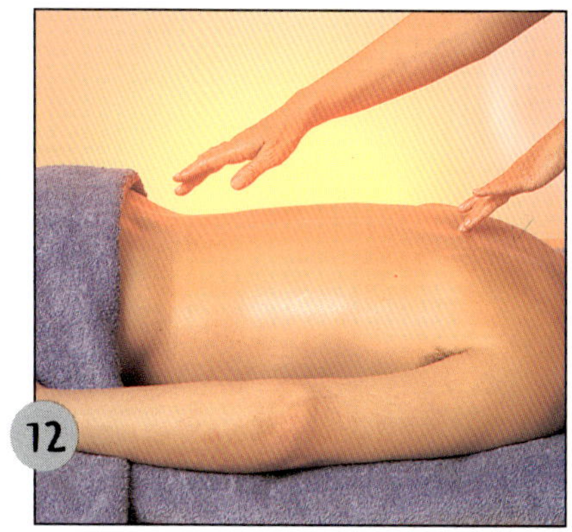

Feather stroke from the base of the spine to the neck, again with an increasingly lighter touch. Ask your partner to turn over on to the back and rearrange the towels.

Neck and Shoulders

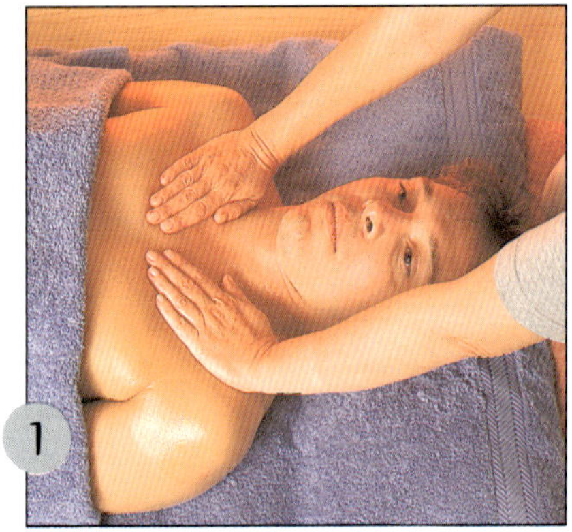

Uncover the neck and shoulders. Lay your hands flat on either side of the upper chest and simply hold them still for a few moments.

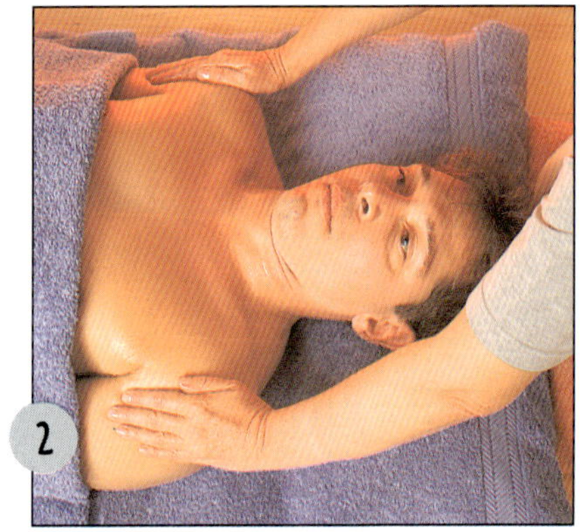

Effleurage firmly over the chest and out under the shoulders, then back up to the neck, pulling out the muscles as you do so. Repeat several times.

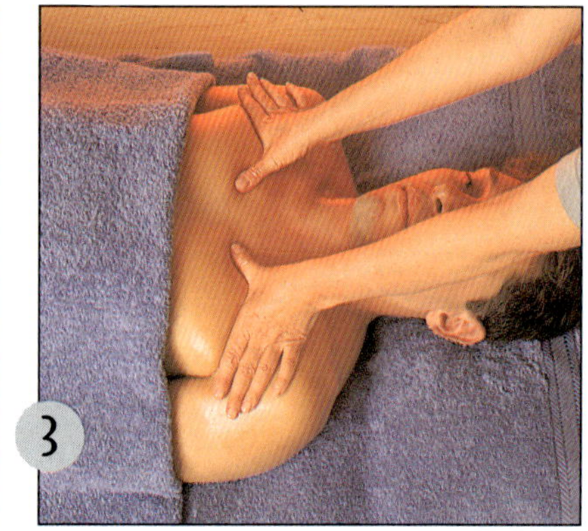

Petrissage the upper chest using the thumbs. Use a firm touch and move gradually downwards.

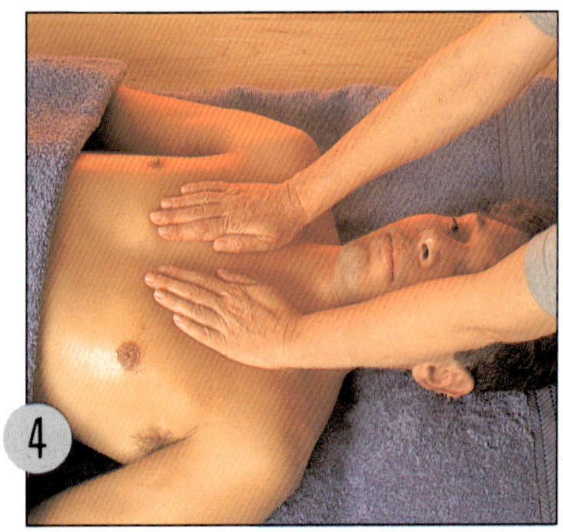

Uncover the chest and effleurage around the breasts with a firm, circular movement.

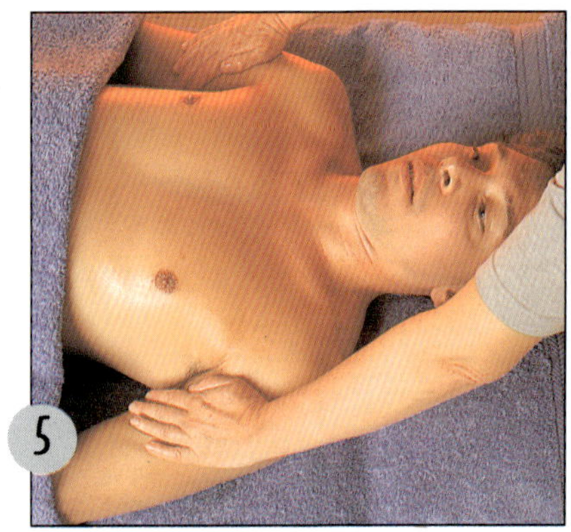

Enlarge the circle so that the hands travel out over the arms, returning up the back and coming over the shoulders.

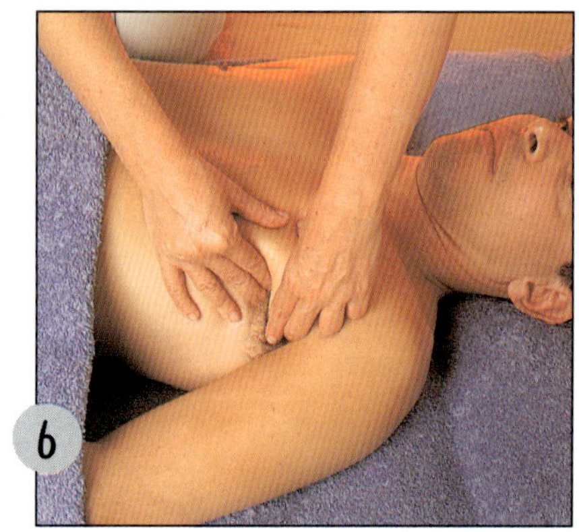

Knead the upper chest where the breast meets the armpit. Effleurage the whole area with increasing lightness of touch. Cover the chest and uncover the right arm.

ARMS, HANDS AND WRIST

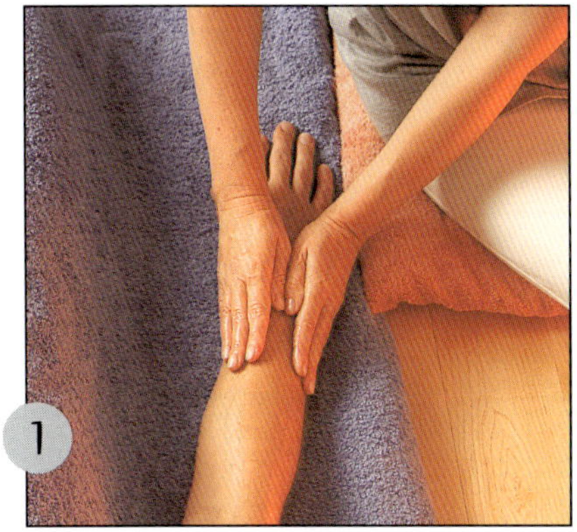

Hold the wrist in one hand and lift the arm away from the floor or bed – it should be a dead weight, with no effort made by your partner. Place your hands either side of the wrist.

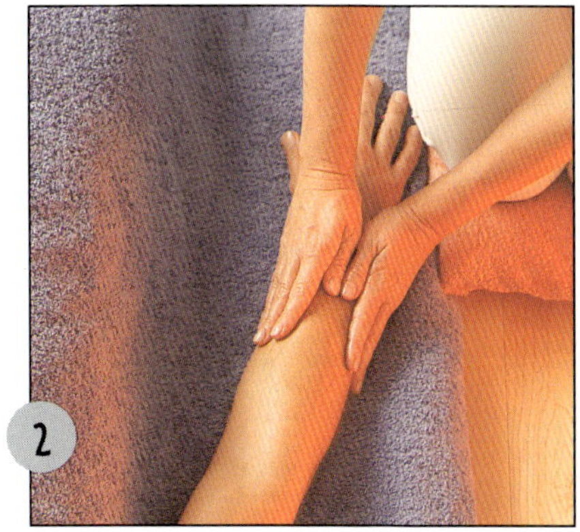

Effleurage from the wrist to the top of the arm using a firm pressure.

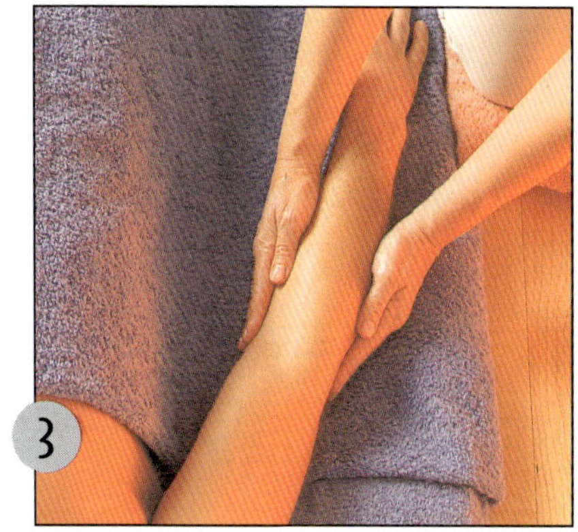

For the return movement, take the hands to the outside of the arm and sweep downwards. Repeat several times.

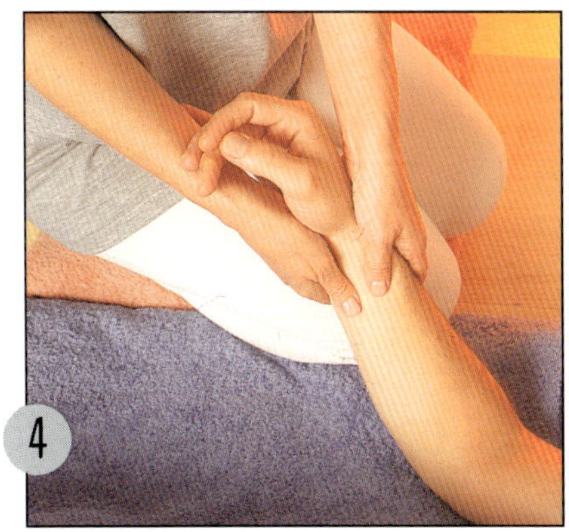

Bend the arm at the elbow with the palm uppermost. Petrissage from the wrist to the elbow, coming back down to the wrist each time in a smooth effleurage stroke. Repeat several times.

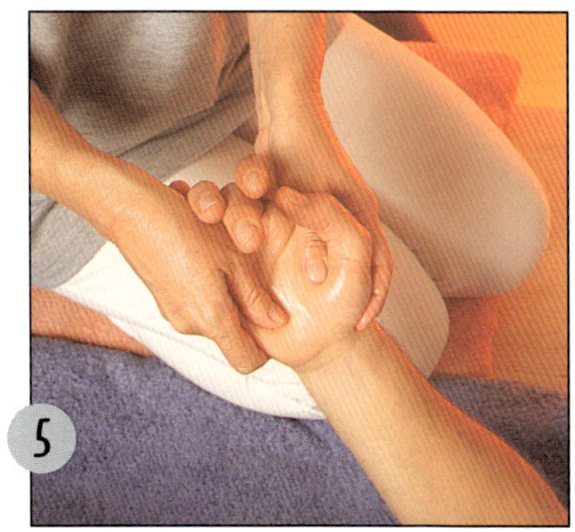

Petrissage the palm of the hand, then turn it over and petrissage very gently between the fingers.

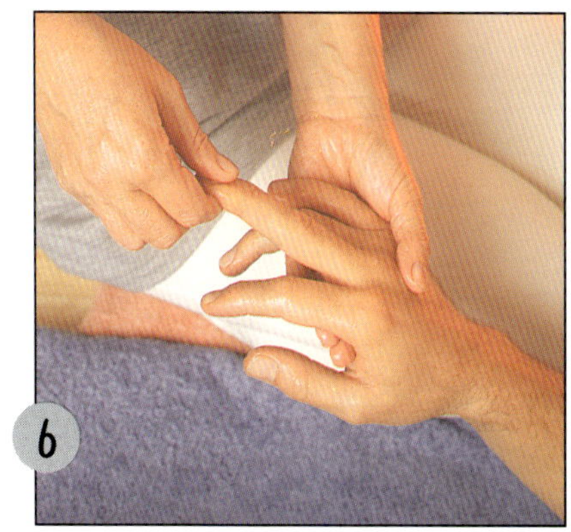

Pull each finger gently to stretch it out. Effleurage the arm as at the beginning several times. Cover it and repeat for the other arm.

Abdomen

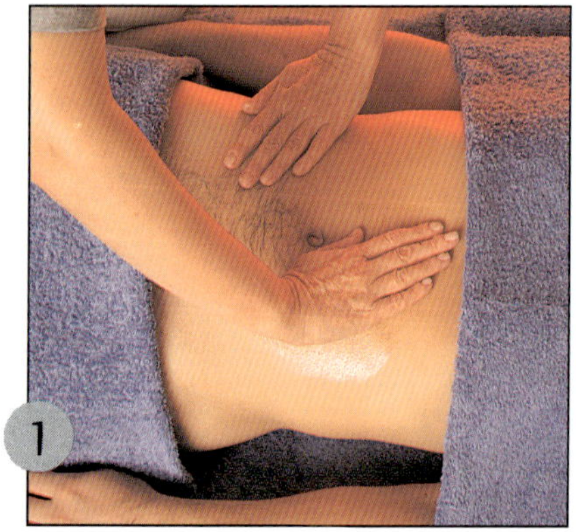

Uncover the abdomen and effleurage the whole area gently. If there is any pain here, stop immediately and do not use much pressure in any case as this area is very sensitive.

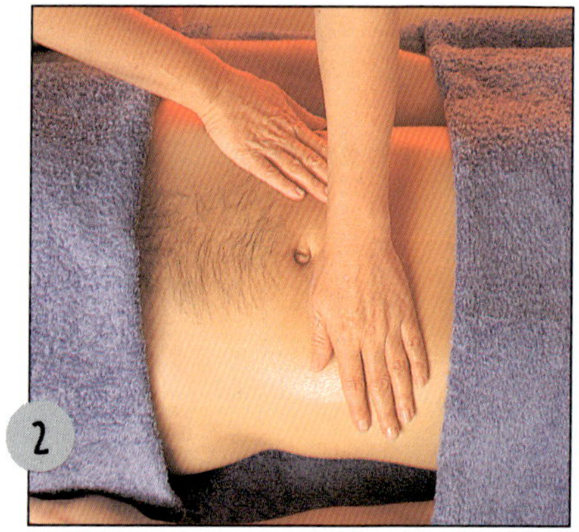

Effleurage the whole abdomen with a circular movement, one hand following the other.

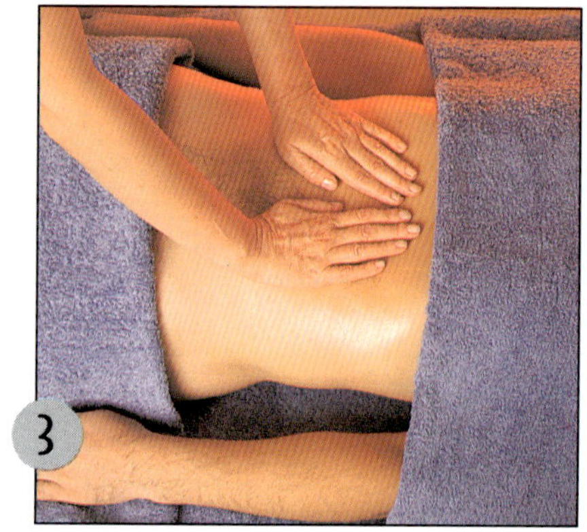

Starting with the palms together in the centre of the abdomen, move them gradually apart towards the sides of the body.

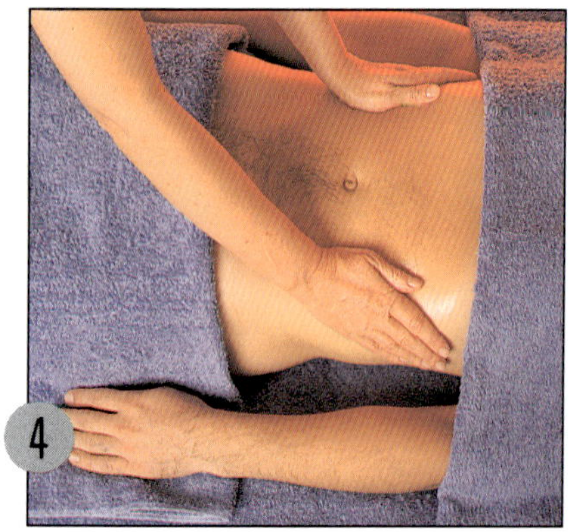

Let your hands glide out over the sides and under the back so that they meet at the spine.

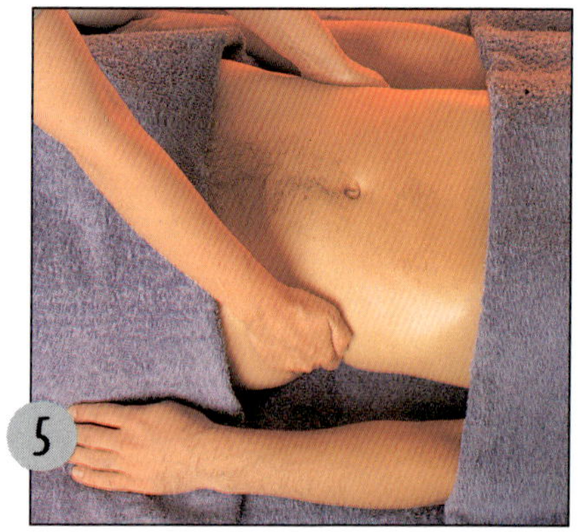

When your fingers touch beneath the back, start to draw them back, pulling out the back muscles gently as you go. Repeat several times.

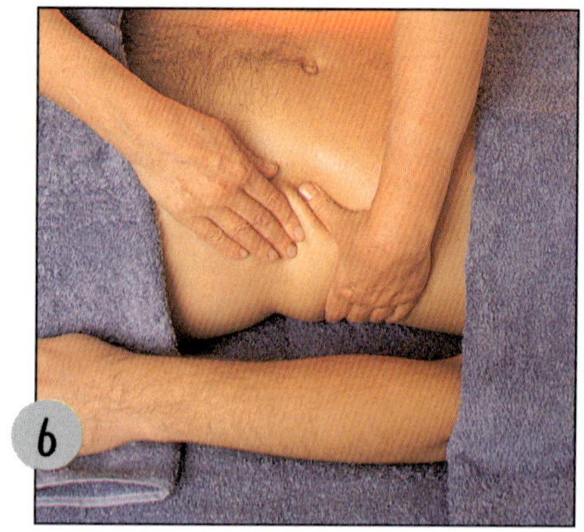

Knead one side of the abdomen, then effleurage gently. Swap sides. Cover the abdomen.

FOOT, LEG AND ANKLE

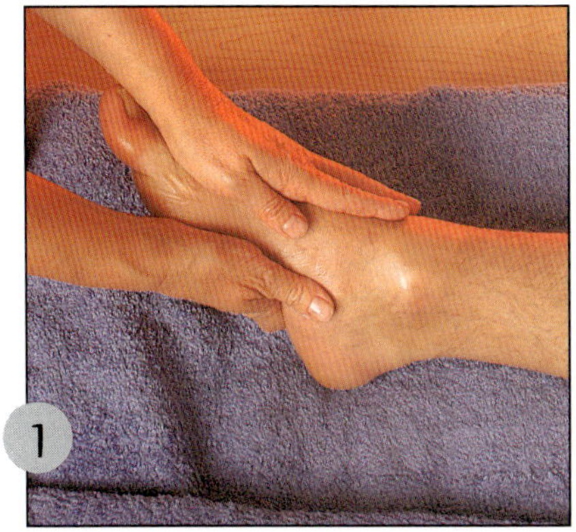

Uncover the right leg. Having warmed the oil in your palms, gently effleurage the whole of the foot.

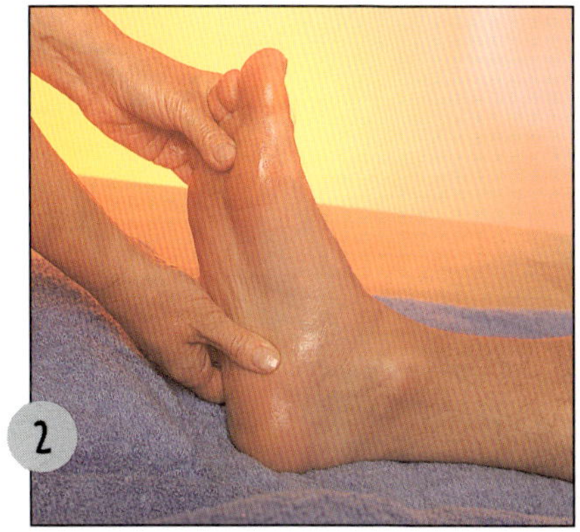

Petrissage the sole of the foot. If you use a firm pressure, this should not make your partner ticklish!

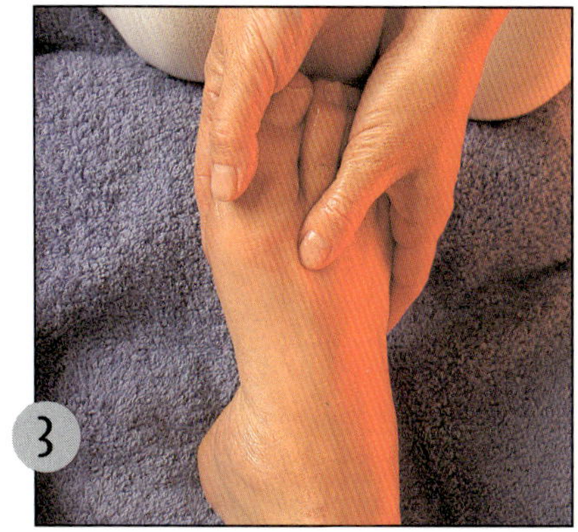

Petrissage between the toes, then pull out and gently stretch each toe.

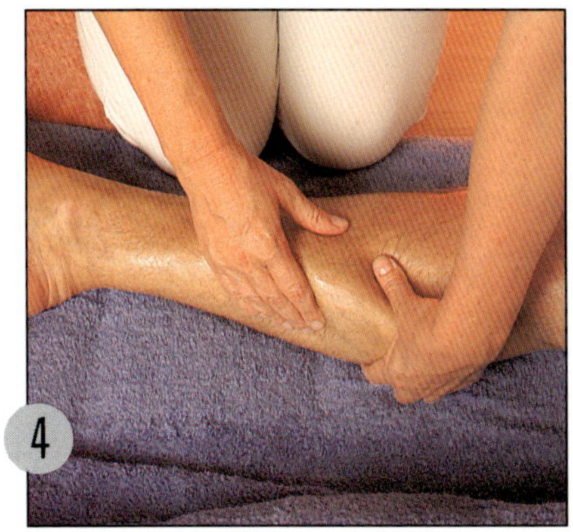

Knead the calf muscle. Effleurage from ankle to groin, up the centre and back down the sides gently. Repeat several times. Then petrissage from the upper knee to the groin. Repeat several times.

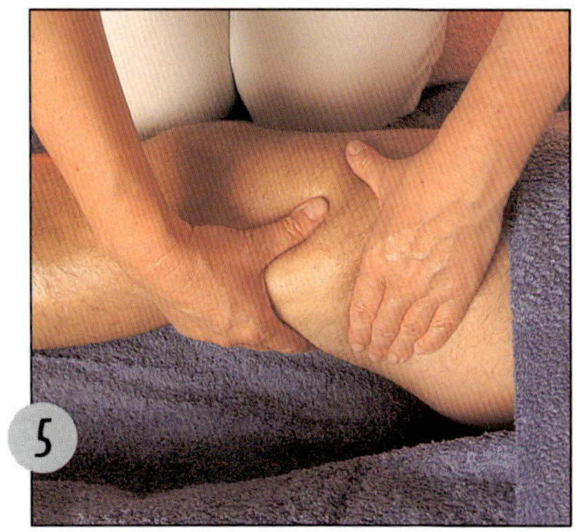

Knead the upper leg. Then alternate effleurage the whole of the upper leg. Repeat several times. Effleurage the whole leg. Cover and repeat on the left. When you have finished, cover your partner except for the feet.

SOLE OF FOOT

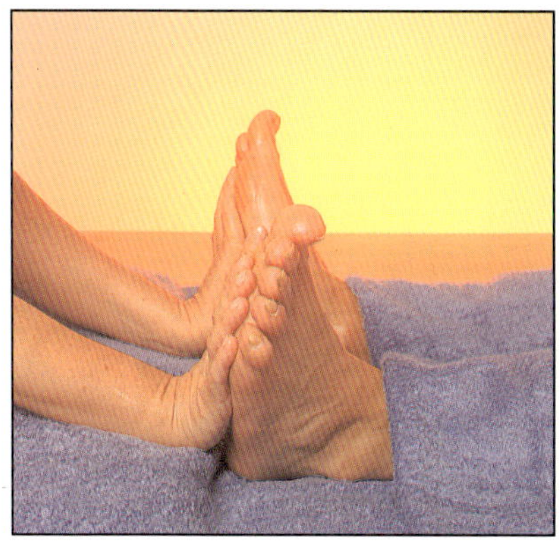

Place your palms on the soles of the feet and hold them there for at least a minute. Cover the feet and leave your partner to relax for a few minutes. Wash your hands and arms in cold water to remove negative energy.

SPECIFIC APPLICATIONS

There are a number of conditions that respond particularly well to treatment by aromatherapy. These include stress and emotional problems such as depression and insomnia, respiratory conditions, especially coughs and colds, and some digestive, muscular and skin conditions. It can also be used as first first aid for several minor emergencies. However, it is very important to recognize that aromatherapy, though very successful in some areas, has its limitations. More serious conditions – or potentially serious ones – must be treated by a doctor. The underlying rule is – if in doubt, always consult a doctor or, in an emergency, a hospital.

The uses and properties of all the aromatherapy oils are extremely complex. If you are worried by a particular condition and you decide you want to try treating it with essential oils, it is probably best in the first instance to consult a trained aromatherapist (see page 62). Nevertheless, aromatherapy can be a very useful form of home treatment and, in the following pages, various conditions are given with aromatherapy "recipes". There is often more than one method of treating a problem – by massage or as a bath, for example. In some cases, I have given actual recipes, in others, the many oils that are beneficial for a particular condition. This gives you the basis to experiment, blending oils to produce an aroma that you like, which very often proves to be the very oil that is most beneficial. So, trust in your instincts and be creative!

A number of ailments respond well to aromatherapy oils whether used in massage, bath and compresses or when inhaled.

STRESS AND EMOTIONAL PROBLEMS

pages 42-44

Aromatherapy is widely recognized as an effective means of dealing with stress, particularly when combined with massage. It is also useful for other ailments which may result from an emotional cause, such as depression and insomnia.

RESPIRATORY PROBLEMS

pages 45-47

Many respiratory complaints may be relieved by inhaling essential oils, either a few drops on a pillow or tissue or as a steam inhalation. You can also massage the affected area yourself if you have a sore throat or bronchitis.

MUSCULAR AND CIRCULATORY PROBLEMS

pages 48-50

Compresses using aromatherapy oils can be particularly soothing, especially for sufferers from arthritis and rheumatism or anyone who has pain and inflammation resulting from injury.

DIGESTIVE PROBLEMS

pages 51-52

The digestive system is a delicate mechanism and, for many people, one that is particularly prone to upset. Aromatherapy oils may be useful in a wide variety of ways – from calming indigestion to relieving a hangover.

WOMEN, PREGNANCY AND CHILDBIRTH

pages 53-55

A whole range of problems that apply specifically to women – such as PMT, menstrual cramps and cystitis – may be effectively alleviated with essential oils. They may also prove beneficial in overcoming the side-effects experienced during pregnancy – like heartburn and morning sickness – but always check the oils to avoid in pregnancy first (see right).

SKIN AND HAIR

pages 56-58

Many skin complaints may benefit from treatment with essential oils – such as acne and eczema. Hair and scalp problems may also be improved, particularly dandruff and head lice – a common problem for schoolchildren.

CHILDREN'S PROBLEMS

page 59

Babies and children find aromatherapy oils very calming and soothing. Often the best method for them is a few drops on a pillow or in the bath. However, if applied to the skin, always use the dosages on page 22 as young skin is very sensitive.

FIRST AID

pages 60-61

In minor emergencies, an essential oil first aid kit may prove invaluable. The oils are all antiseptic and many have soothing and healing properties to ease burns, aches, stings and grazes.

WARNING

There are certain contra-indications to be considered when using essential oils. For certain people or particular conditions, some oils must be avoided. These can be divided into the following groups.

Not to be used except by professional therapists

Aniseed; bay; camphor; carrot seed; hyssop; lemon grass; pennyroyal; sage; savory; tarragon; thuja; thyme; wintergreen.

Not to be used on the skin

Cinnamon (bark or leaf); cloves; rue.

Not to be used in pregnancy

Angelica; basil; cinnamon bark; clary *sage; hyssop; juniper berry; lovage; myrrh; origanum; pennyroyal; rosemary; sage; savory; sweet fennel; sweet marjoram; thyme.*

Children – only use the following oils

Camomile; clary sage; eucalyptus; geranium; juniper berry; lavender; peppermint; rose; rosemary; sage; sandalwood; sweet marjoram; tea tree.

Stress and Emotional Problems

One of the areas in which aromatherapy can be most advantageous is for stress and emotional problems. The oils are particularly effective for these problems when used in conjunction with a full body massage (see pages 26-39), though as a room perfume, on a pillow, in the bath or as a partial self-massage they can also prove beneficial.

Fatigue and Nervous Exhaustion

Too many responsibilities – work, looking after children, running a home – and not enough time for yourself, can leave you feeling it takes all your energy just to get through the day. If you do feel this way, you should try to get as much rest as possible, eat a good diet and take regular gentle exercise – though, of course, this is easier said than done if you are starting with an impossible schedule. For an instant lift, basil oil is extremely stimulating. Used in an early morning bath or simply inhaled from a tissue during the course of the day, it can give you a boost. Rosemary, peppermint and clary sage are also good, especially if used in the mornings. Stimulating oils should be avoided at night when you need your rest. Lavender on the pillow at night helps promote a sound sleep. One of the baths or massages suggested for anxiety or insomnia is also a good way of revving down your system in the evening and preparing yourself for a good night's sleep.

Clary sage

Anxiety and Tension

Emotional tension and anxiety can hardly fail to lead to physical tension. This may result in headaches (see page 44), palpitations, various digestive disorders, such as diarrhoea and nausea, insomnia and any number of other unexplained pains and problems – not to mention the possibility of long-term illnesses such as ulcers or heart disease.

The physical contact of a full body massage combined with uplifting and calming oils can help to promote much-needed relaxation. Some of the best oils for this purpose are ylang-ylang, geranium, rose, neroli, melissa, lavender, sandalwood and patchouli. A mixture of two or three favourites can be used for a full massage by an aromatherapist or a friend, or you can use them to give yourself a mini-massage, put them in the bath or inhale them from a tissue by day or from your pillow at night.

The heady fragrances of many of the aromatherapy oils will subtly change moods when used as room fragrances.

Rose or jasmine oil inhaled from a handkerchief can help to lift the spirits.

Depression

There are times when everyone feels depressed. This is often a fairly short-lived feeling but it can develop into a chronic problem that seems impossible to overcome. Most people nowadays regard anti-depressant drugs as something to be avoided at all costs and prefer to look for help elsewhere. With long-term depression, counselling may be the answer. To balance your emotional state and help you to feel able to cope, a full body massage with uplifting and relaxing oils can be beneficial. Simply the fact that it is a very pleasurable treat may help in itself. Good oils are jasmine, clary sage, ylang-ylang, bergamot, neroli, rose, orange, lemon and lavender. Any of these oils will work well in the bath, too, and you can sprinkle a few drops of jasmine or rose on a tissue to inhale during the day.

Insomnia

Insomnia is a common result of stress and there is nothing more frustrating than lying awake for hours, knowing you are going to feel exhausted the next, inevitably busy, day. Worrying about it, of course, only makes sleep more impossible.

Take time to wind down at the end of the day. Avoid stimulants such as coffee and don't eat too late in the evening. Lavender, neroli, rose and sweet marjoram are among the best oils for insomnia. They can be used for a full body massage, as a self-massage of the face, neck and shoulders, or in the bath for a good, long soak. A few drops of lavender or neroli on your pillow is an excellent sedative and soporific.

Low Sex-drive

A low sex drive is a common result of fatigue, stress or anxiety. It is possible to redress the sexual balance with a combination of a relaxing massage with a heady essential oil that has euphoric qualities. The best oils are rose, ylang-ylang, clary sage, patchouli, jasmine and sandalwood, either one alone or two or three mixed together according to your own preference. You could also use one of these oils to scent a room in a vaporizer.

In today's stress-filled world, many emotionally-based problems may take hold, often causing physical side-effects.

HEADACHES AND MIGRAINE

Headaches can result from stress, poor diet, hormonal disturbances, allergies or various other factors. You should consult your doctor about severe, recurrent headaches. If it is a mild headache resulting from stress, sitting too long at your desk or being in a noisy, smoky atmosphere, it may vanish simply by massaging a few drops of neat lavender oil into your temples and the back of your neck. Inhaling peppermint oil can sometimes bring relief, especially when massage would be painful. A neck and shoulder massage or a bath with peppermint, sweet marjoram or melissa can also be beneficial.

Stress headaches may be relieved simply by massaging neat lavender oil into the painful area.

A more thorough self-massage for headache and migraine is possible. Start at the centre of the forehead, at the hairline.

With gentle circular movements, follow the hairline around to the temples and massage this area for a few moments.

Then, continuing along the hairline, move around to the back of the neck with the same circular motion. Repeat the whole process several times.

Respiratory Problems

Because of the naturally antiseptic qualities of essential oils, their inhalation has a particularly strong and immediate effect on problems of the respiratory system. You should also make a few simple changes to your diet. If you have a cold, cough, sore throat or flu, avoid dairy products as they produce mucus, thus aggravating the symptoms and making breathing more difficult. Avoid smoky atmospheres and, if you yourself smoke – stop!

Colds and Flu

Eucalyptus is a very important oil for problems of the respiratory tract. It is an antiseptic and decongestant, so a drop on a tissue during the day or on your pillow at night can help you to breathe and get rid of stuffiness. (It is the active ingredient in many proprietary decongestants.) An inhalation of 4 drops each of tea tree and eucalyptus oils and 2 drops of peppermint in steam should be taken three or four times a day.

Lavender used as a room freshener has a naturally antiseptic effect, too. Gargling regularly with a drop of tea tree oil in water is a good preventative to ward off colds.

Eucalyptus

Coughs

A good mixture of oils to inhale for a cough is 4 drops each of cypress and juniper with 2 drops of ginger. For a dry cough, substitute cedarwood and camomile for the first two ingredients.

For many respiratory problems, simply inhaling an essential oil from a tissue may bring speedy relief.

Catarrh and Sinusitis

The most common method of treatment is by steam inhalation using a mixture of 2 drops of lemon (or peppermint) oil and 4 drops each of eucalyptus and lavender oils.

You can also put the same mixture on a tissue and breathe it in regularly throughout the day. Lastly, you can try a very gentle face massage, concentrating on the brow and cheekbones. Make up a blend of 10 drops of lavender, 6 drops of eucalyptus and 9 drops of peppermint in carrier oil and apply sparingly.

The symptoms of colds and flu, catarrh and sinusitis can all be relieved by steam inhalation.

Sore Throats and Throat Infections

Gargling with 2 drops of each of tea tree and sandalwood oil in water may help to fight off a throat infection as well as bring local pain relief. It also helps laryngitis. You can apply a massage oil to the throat, face and chest – or, better still, ask someone else to massage it for you. Mix 9 drops each of sandalwood and clary sage oils with 7 drops of ginger. You can substitute eucalyptus and peppermint for other oils in the mixture.

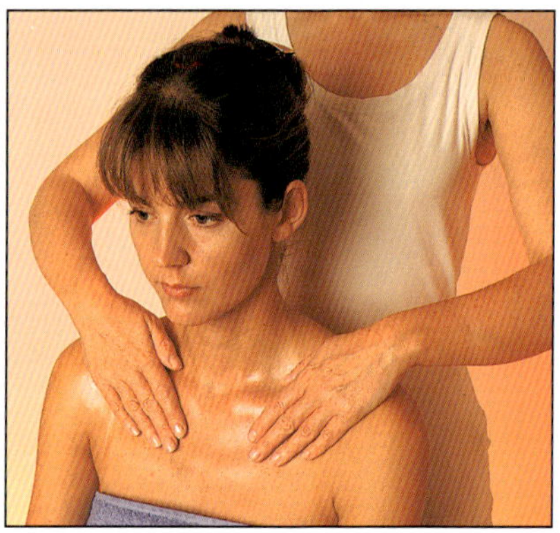

Using one of the blends mentioned left, stand behind your partner and put your hands flat on the top of the chest. Leave them there for a minute, then make long sweeping strokes across and up the chest.

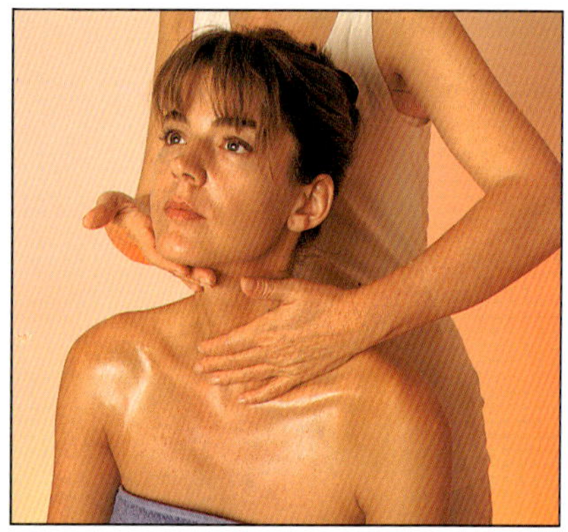

Continue the strokes up the throat towards the chin. When you have finished, wrap your partner up in towels to rest for half an hour while the oil is absorbed into the skin.

TONSILLITIS

Consult a doctor about an attack of tonsillitis whether in adults or children. A steam inhalation with bergamot may bring some relief for adults.

Bergamot

EARACHE

Sinusitis can cause earache as a side-effect. A compress of either lavender or camomile laid over the painful area should bring relief.

Use natural cotton fabric to make a compress. Soak it in hot water to which lavender or camomile oil has been added and apply it to the skin for at least one hour.

ASTHMA

Again, consult your doctor about this problem. However, you can try inhaling from a tissue – though not over steam – a few drops of lavender, sage eucalyptus or frankincense oil. You can experiment to find a blend that suits you and use the same mixture in carrier oil for massage, which feels especially good on the chest and back.

BRONCHITIS

Consult your doctor about bronchitis. For temporary relief, try a steam inhalation of 4 drops each of cedarwood and eucalyptus oils with 2 drops of sandalwood. You can also massage the chest and throat with the same oils diluted in carrier oil in the proportion 10:10:5.

Cedarwood, eucalyptus or sandalwood oils are suitable for the temporary relief from bronchitis.

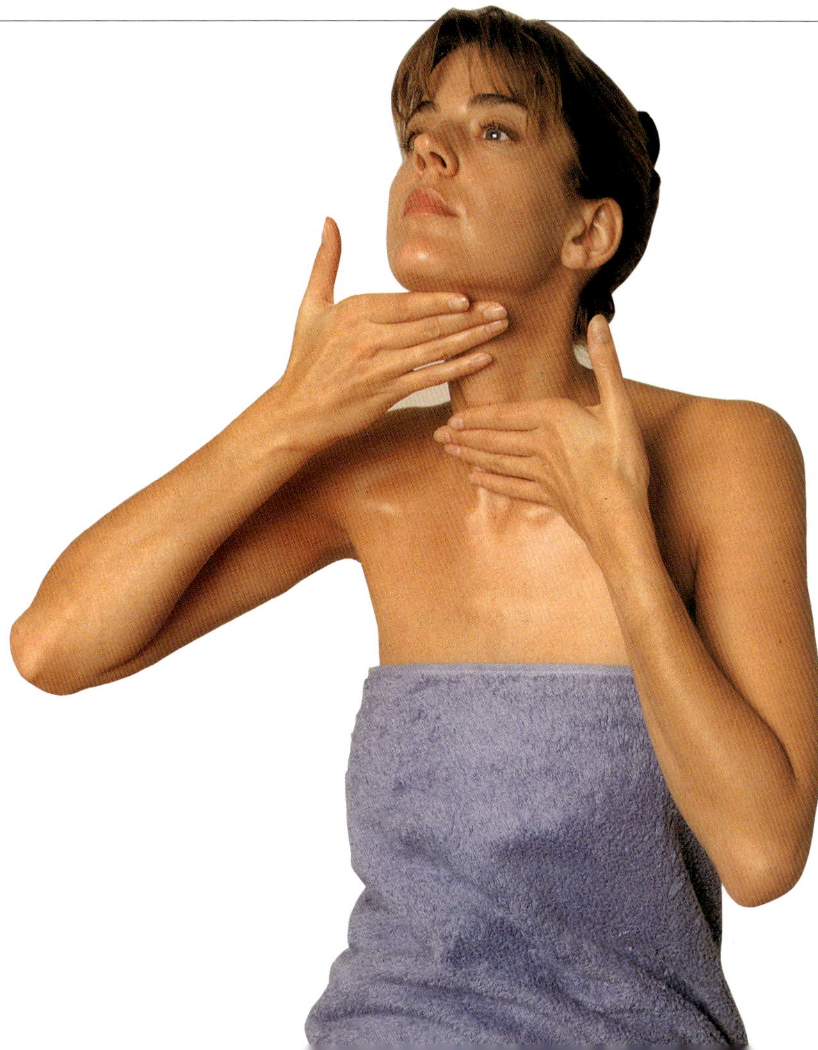

A chest and throat massage with cedarwood, eucalyptus and sandalwood oils will relieve the uncomfortable symptoms of bronchitis.

MUSCULAR AND CIRCULATORY PROBLEMS

Backache is one of the commonest problems in western society. It can be the result of injury, poor posture, weak supporting muscles, even stress. Sports injuries are another common complaint and both respond well to essential oils, especially when they are combined with massage.

Rheumatism and arthritis are problems we usually associate with the elderly but, in fact, they can affect people of any age, including children. If there is pain or inflammation, avoid massage, however, and use compresses or baths instead.

Many essential oils can be added to the bath to give either a relaxing or stimulating effect.

RHEUMATISM AND ARTHRITIS

Rheumatism is the lay term for pain and stiffness in the muscles and joints; arthritis for pain and swelling in the joints; osteoarthritis, a degenerative disease of the joints, wears away the protective cartilage often of the fingers, knees, hips and spine. There can be severe pain and swelling leading to immobility. Aromatherapy is helpful as a pain relief and muscle relaxant. If joints are swollen and painful, baths and compresses should be used instead of massage. Try a blend of two or three of these oils as a compress or in a bath – camomile, pine, eucalyptus, lavender, juniper, ginger, rosemary, lemon and sweet marjoram. If massage would not be painful – and inflamed joints must *always* be avoided – a blend of 10 drops each of rosemary and frankincense with 5 drops of eucalyptus can be made with half the usual amount of carrier oil (ie 25ml).

MUSCULAR ACHES AND PAINS (INCLUDING BACKACHE)

These may be general aches and pains caused by physical exertion (perhaps in sport), extreme tiredness or a side-effect of another ailment such as flu. Alternatively, you may have a long-term back problem resulting from an old injury or because of postural problems. If the latter is the cause, consider yoga or Alexander technique as a long-term option.

Massage may be beneficial in all of these cases but it should be very gentle, particularly if there is any inflammation or a muscle is tensed. Remember that, in back massage, the spine itself is not touched – only massage at its sides.

You can massage the afflicted area or have a whole body massage with a mixture of 12 drops of ginger, 5 drops of juniper and 8 drops of rosemary or lavender (rosemary is more invigorating, lavender more soothing). A bath or a compress using camomile, lavender, juniper, eucalyptus or rosemary may also be beneficial.

Rosemary

CRAMP

This may be a result of physical exertion, in which case the treatment is the same as for muscular aches and pains. Some people, however, suffer from long-term recurrent cramp. I treated one elderly man who would wake several times every night with cramp in his feet and legs. He found that a twice-weekly foot massage gave him an uninterrupted sleep and no pain. I used a mixture of 10 drops each of lavender and rosemary and 5 drops of sweet marjoram.

Sweet marjoram

While regular exercise has an overall beneficial effect, there is always the risk of injury or just general aches and pains resulting from unaccustomed exertion. Baths and massage can both be of help in different circumstances.

Poor Circulation and Low Blood Pressure

Circulation can be improved by taking gentle exercise and also by deep breathing exercises. Massage and baths with essential oils may also be beneficial and stimulating essences such as juniper, cypress, black pepper, rosemary, orange and lemon are recommended. Mix two or three together according to your personal preference.

Varicose Veins and Haemorrhoids

Varicose veins often occur during pregnancy, but they do affect both men and women, the veins in the legs becoming swollen and knotted. Walking as often as possible is recommended. Haemorrhoids are varicose veins that occur inside or outside the anus. They can be painful and bleed during a bowel movement. Constipation (page 52) is a common cause.

Warm (not hot) baths with cypress oil are recommended for both problems. For varicose veins, a blend of cypress, lemon and lime can be used as a massage oil. Sandalwood may also be used.

Cypress

Exercise, especially when taken in the fresh air, improves circulation, as well as having an overall stimulating effect.

High Blood Pressure

High blood pressure can also be improved by making some adjustments to your day-to-day habits. Cutting out smoking and heavy drinking, and changing to a healthier diet may all help, as may relaxation techniques if you are suffering from stress. You should also consult your doctor. Aromatherapy is particularly useful in this context as a whole body massage to facilitate deep relaxation, using oils such as ylang-ylang, lavender, lemon and sweet marjoram – two or three mixed according to personal preference.

DIGESTIVE PROBLEMS

The digestive system is a delicate mechanism for many people and the place in which symptoms of stress manifest themselves – especially nausea and diarrhoea. Constipation is an extremely widespread problem in western societies – principally due to diet.

Large quantities of fresh (preferably raw) fruit and vegetables, together with drinking plenty of water, are basic essentials for a good diet and a healthy digestive system.

INDIGESTION, NAUSEA AND FLATULENCE

One of the best oils for digestive problems is peppermint. For indigestion, nausea or flatulence, drink a glass of honey water with 4 drops added. Alternatively, for indigestion, you could gently massage a blend of 10 drops each of peppermint and ginger and 5 drops of lemon in 50ml of carrier oil into the abdomen. Peppermint and camomile herbal teas are also useful.

Peppermint and camomile tea may help relieve symptoms of digestive problems.

MOUTH ULCERS

Mouth ulcers can appear on the gums, cheeks or along the edges of the tongue because of stomach upsets or poor diet. However, they often occur as a result of stress, too. You can apply oils neat to them or use a mouthwash. If applying directly, every 3 or 4 hours, alternate with 1 drop of myrrh or tea tree oil on a cotton bud.

As a mouthwash, you can mix together 1 drop each of tea tree, geranium, lavender and lemon oils in a glass of water and use every 2 hours.

Apply neat tea tree or myrrh oil directly on to the mouth ulcer with a cotton bud for relief from symptoms.

HANGOVER

If you wake up with a hangover, the most important aid to recovery is water – drink plenty of it and add 1 drop of rose or peppermint oil to each glass, and a teaspoon of honey. A compress using geranium oil may help a thumping head and, for a restorative bath, add 2 drops each of lavender and juniper oils and 1 drop of rosemary.

Geranium

Drink plenty of water when you have a hangover, adding just one drop of rose or peppermint oil and a teaspoon of honey.

CONSTIPATION

Constipation must be addressed taking overall diet, fibre intake and exercise into consideration and you may need to consult your doctor if this is a long-term problem. If you suffer occasionally from mild constipation, this is a useful blend to massage into the lower back, buttocks and abdomen: 10 drops each of marjoram and rosemary, 5 drops of black pepper.

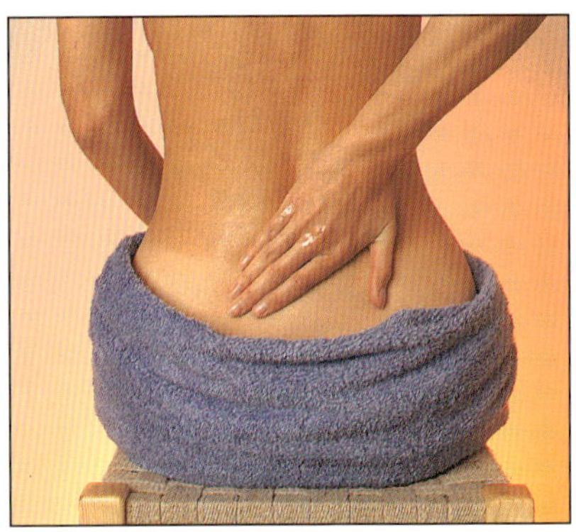

Massaging the lower back with a marjoram, rosemary and black pepper blend can be useful for mild constipation.

DIARRHOEA

Diarrhoea can result from a number of causes – anything from stress to food poisoning. It can even be a side-effect of jetlag. See your doctor if the problem lasts for more than a day or so. You may find a bath with 2 drops of geranium, juniper berry and peppermint oils added will ease the problem. Alternatively, massage the abdomen very gently in a clockwise direction with a blend of 5 drops each of peppermint, tea tree, sandalwood and geranium oils in the usual 50ml of carrier oil. This can also be rubbed gently into the lower back.

Women, Pregnancy and Childbirth

The delicacy and complexity of the female reproductive system leaves it open to many problems and few women manage to get through life without suffering from period pains, PMT or unpleasant menopausal symptoms. Much of this may be relieved by the use of aromatherapy oils. Many of the side-effects of pregnancy, too, may be alleviated – such problems as stretchmarks, nausea in the mornings, backache (see page 49) and heartburn. However, great care must be taken with essential oils during pregnancy – check the list on page 41 before use.

Menstrual Cramps

Many women suffer from painful period cramps and often experience up to 48 hours of misery. The best mixture I have found is an oil made up of 5 drops each of camomile and geranium and 15 drops of clary sage. Sweet marjoram can also be used but the most important oil in the mixture is the clary sage. Massage the oil into the abdomen on the flat of your hand in a circular motion (going clockwise as you look down). You may also find it effective to massage some of the oil into the small of the back.

You can take clary sage oil internally as well, using 3 drops in a glass of water.

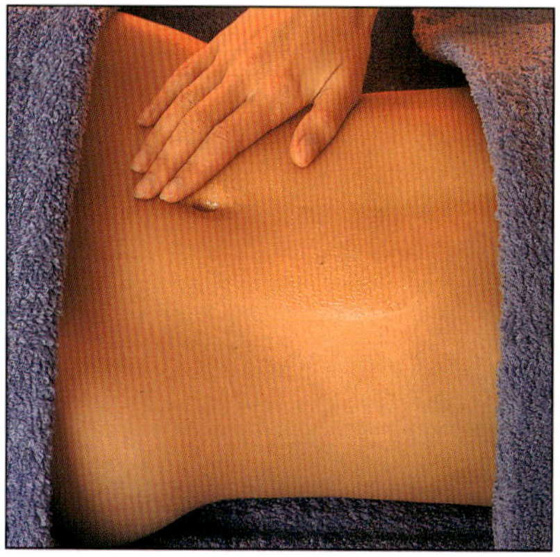

A gentle massage – in a clockwise direction – of the abdomen with clary sage, camomile and geranium can be effective in relieving menstrual cramps.

PMT

If you get irritable or depressed just before the onset of your period, the easiest way to calm and uplift the spirits is in a bath to which ylang-ylang and clary sage have been added. If you have an aromatherapist or a friend who can give you a whole body massage, this is better still. Use the same oils in roughly equal proportions.

Cystitis

Caused by an inflammation of the lining of the bladder, cystitis can be a particularly painful and distressing problem. Not only does it make you want to rush to the loo every few minutes, there is a burning sensation when you do urinate.

Internally, you can take one drop of camomile oil in a glass of honey water. You can also take two baths a day (at least) staying in for between 10 and 15 minutes. Add 2 drops of lavender, juniper berry, eucalyptus and sandalwood oils. It is very important to drink as much still mineral water as possible, too.

It is very important to drink as much still mineral water as possible with cystitis. You can also take internally a drop of camomile oil in honey water.

Thrush

The white and sometimes smelly discharge of thrush is a result of the intestinal fungus, *candida albicans*, multiplying out of control. It is a very common problem and many women find it a particularly embarrassing one. Regular baths with 2 drops each of tea tree, myrrh and bergamot oils may bring some relief.

Cellulite

Massage roughly equal proportions of juniper, rosemary and lavender oils into affected areas on the thighs, hips and buttocks. You should use firm strokes, moving upwards from the knee, but no pummelling.

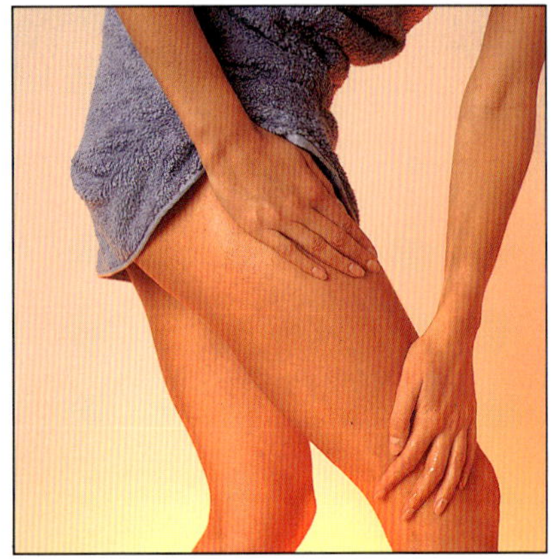

Massage areas of cellulite on a regular daily basis with a blend of juniper, rosemary and lavender oils.

Stretchmarks

Although they are usually associated with pregnancy, stretchmarks can also be caused by extreme overweight. They will never disappear but massaging with a blend of 20 drops of lavender and 5 of neroli (preferably in a rich carrier oil such as wheatgerm or almond) will improve them. This is a good mixture to use from the fourth month of pregnancy as a preventative, too. Apply morning and night to the abdomen, thighs and breasts.

Some of the less pleasant side-effects of pregnancy, such as nausea and heartburn, may be relieved with the help of essential oils.

Pregnancy

During pregnancy, there are certain oils that should not be used. See page 41.

Heartburn

This is a form of indigestion that seems particularly to afflict pregnant women. 1 drop of peppermint or sandalwood oil in water usually brings some relief.

Morning Sickness

Peppermint oil has a very calming effect on the digestive system and one drop in a glass of honey water should help with nausea. Peppermint tea may also bring some relief.

Episiotomy

Many women have an episiotomy (a cut at the bottom of the vagina) during labour or a tear caused by pushing out the baby. Even if you have suffered neither of these, you may still be feeling very sore. Lavender oil in the bath is very soothing and also speeds up the healing process.

Lavender

Labour

Massage of the lower back can bring great relief during a long labour. A mixture of 15 drops of lavender oil and 5 drops each of rose and ylang-ylang should also help relaxation and lift the spirits when you are feeling exhausted. Ask a partner, friend or midwife to massage the lower back with firm, upward-sweeping strokes.

Aromatherapy oils can help relieve menopausal symptoms and allow you to enjoy your maturity to the full.

Menopause

The two most common problems women suffer during the menopause are hot flushes and mood swings or depression. Baths with 4 drops of clary sage oil and 2 each of peppermint and geranium are recommended. For hot flushes, try inhaling some peppermint oil on a tissue. A whole body massage using roughly equal proportions of geranium, sandalwood and camomile oils should prove beneficial. Or you can use the same mixture to massage into your neck and throat.

Post-natal depression

On the third or fourth day after birth, the immense hormonal upheavals that are taking place in your body can cause post-natal depression. This can be eased with jasmine or ylang-ylang oil. Use them in the bath or on burners to scent the room.

Jasmine or ylang-ylang essential oils lift the spirits if you are coping with post-natal exhaustion and hormonal changes.

SKIN AND HAIR

The skin readily absorbs essential oils, making them ideal for skin complaints. Many oils can be used in preparations that are cosmetic, too. Use lemon oil if you have oily skin, sandalwood for dry skin and rose or frankincense for mature skin. When using essential oils on the face, you use a weaker dilution than that for the body (see page 24).

ACNE

Spots and acne are most commonly the result of either hormonal imbalance or poor diet – or both. Acne is particularly associated with adolescence but, in fact, spots can occur at any time and many women get them just before menstruation whatever their age. Cutting out junk food and very spicy or fatty foods is imperative and drinking plenty of mineral water is important, too. Don't squeeze spots – this only encourages the sebaceous glands to produce more. Put 5 drops each of lemon, cypress and juniper oils into 50ml (2 fl oz) of water and mix well. Bathe the affected area with this several times a day. At night, you could use the same essential oils mixed in a carrier oil.

Adolescents often suffer from skin problems that may be relieved by antiseptic essential oils, when used in combination with a healthy diet.

COLD SORES (HERPES SIMPLEX)

This very common virus brings blisters around the mouth that burst and sometimes bleed. *If the problem spreads or persists, consult your doctor.* Keep the affected area scrupulously clean, and wash it separately with cotton wool. There should be no contact with any other parts of the face. Adults with cold sores should avoid children – for whom this can be a very painful condition.

Bergamot, eucalyptus and tea tree are all suitable oils. Mix a combination of 2 or 3 of these in carrier oil and apply regularly to the affected area.

If eczema results in broken skin, massage is not advisable. Instead, use a compress of camomile, lavender or geranium.

Eczema

Eczema can stem from a very wide range of causes. It is often hereditary, it can be an allergic reaction and it can be triggered by stress or tiredness. I have suffered from eczema all my life and at one time it was quite bad – my fingers were cracked, swollen and bleeding. I find that plenty of rest (and relief from stress, if possible) combined with a sensible diet (no caffeine or alcohol) clears it up within a week. For localized relief, dab on neat lavender oil every hour and, providing it is a fairly mild attack, the skin heals over in 3–4 hours. This is not, however, recommended if the skin is very broken. Camomile, lavender and geranium are all wonderfully healing and soothing for eczema and juniper is good for weeping eczema. You can use these in the bath, as a compress or as a general massage oil (in carrier oil) especially if your eczema is triggered by stress. *Do not, however, massage over any areas of broken skin.*

Athlete's Foot

Athlete's foot is caused by a fungal growth which thrives in the sort of conditions provided by sweaty socks! Wash the feet frequently and keep them exposed to the air whenever possible. You can dab neat lavender, lemon or tea tree on to the affected area or put any of these oils into a bowl of warm water as a foot bath. You could also use these essential oils in a carrier oil and apply to the whole area at bedtime.

A footbath is soothing and beneficial for athlete's foot if lavender, tea tree or lemon is added to the warm water.

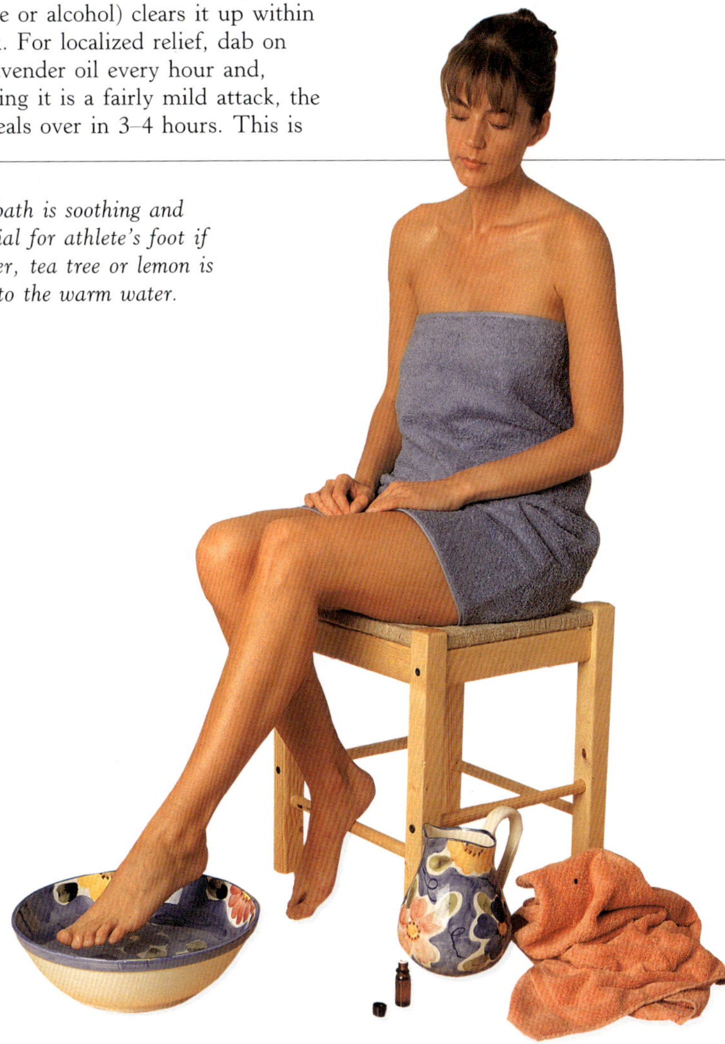

Ringworm

There is no worm involved in ringworm. It is a highly contagious fungal infection that forms a ring on the skin. Treat with 10 drops each of lavender and tea tree oils, and 5 drops of geranium in carrier oil and apply regularly on cotton wool to the affected area.

Dandruff

Dandruff can affect both dry and oily scalps and it requires regular, frequent treatments before you will see an improvement. For an overnight treatment to use two or three times a week, blend 10 drops each of eucalyptus and rosemary oils and 5 drops of juniper or tea tree in 50ml (2 fl oz) of carrier oil. Apply generously all over the hair and scalp and cover in cling film. Next morning, shampoo thoroughly and use the same blend of essential oils in warm water (rather than carrier oil) as a final rinse.

Tea Tree

Head Lice

Outbreaks of head lice are not uncommon in schools. The head louse lays its eggs at the base of the hair shaft and can cause discomfort and even infection of the scalp. Massage a blend of 6 drops of rosemary or tea tree oil, 5 of eucalyptus or geranium and 6 of lavender in 50ml (2 fl oz) of carrier oil into the scalp. The hair should be completely covered, then wrapped in a towel or in cling film. The mixture can be left on for up to 2 hours. Comb through and wash the hair thoroughly (you will need a lot of shampoo to get rid of all the oil). Repeat on a daily basis until the problem has cleared up.

Aromatherapy oils may be very beneficial for problems affecting the hair and scalp, including dandruff, hair loss and head lice.

Hair Loss

Hair loss can be sudden and temporary – after giving birth, as a result of shock or stress, as a side-effect to illness or drugs – or it can be simple male-pattern baldness. In the former cases, the following massage oil will encourage regrowth. In the latter, it may help to slow down the inevitable.

Mix 10 drops each of rosemary and lavender oils plus 5 drops of sandalwood in carrier oil and massage deeply into the scalp. Leave on for at least an hour, then shampoo.

Children's Problems

Children respond very quickly to essential oils and require much weaker doses than adults. As a general rule, do not give children under 10 any oil to be taken internally and, for children over 10, halve the adult dose. With oils to be applied externally, halve the adult dose for children over 5. For younger children and babies. it should be only a quarter of the adult dose. Use only the oils listed here or on page 18 or 41.

Sleep Problems

A drop of lavender on the quilt will help a baby or child to sleep. If a cold and a stuffy nose is preventing sleep, a drop of eucalyptus will clear the head. *Never apply these to the child's skin, only to the bedding.*

A drop of lavender on the pillow will promote a deeper sleep.

Colic

Young babies often suffer a bout of stomach pain, known as colic, at a regular time every day, often, though not always, in the early evening. A warm camomile compress is very soothing and often the baby will fall asleep with it on. Make a compress by soaking a flannel in warm water with 1 drop of camomile oil. Squeeze out the water and lay it over the baby's stomach, then cover with a blanket. Do the same for young children with stomach aches.

Nappy Rash

If your baby has severe, long-lasting nappy rash, it may be because an infection has set in and *in this case you should consult your doctor*. If it seems to be a mild case, however, put 1 drop of lavender oil in the baby's bath. If the skin is not broken, you could also apply a mixture of 4 drops of lavender and 2 of camomile in 50ml (2 fl oz) of carrier oil. You will need only a tiny amount at a time and, of course, you should apply it very gently. You could also use this mixture as a preventative.

Tears and Tantrums

Young children are extremely prone to tears and tantrums, whether from frustration or nerves. A drop of lavender, clary sage or geranium oil, preferably in the bath or, alternatively, on their clothes, can often calm them.

Teething

A drop of lavender or camomile oil on the baby's pyjamas or bedding will be calming and soothing.

First Aid

There are some oils that may bring instant relief in minor emergencies. If symptoms persist, however, or for more severe accidents, always consult a doctor or hospital.

These are some of the occasions when neat oils may be applied. The most useful oil is lavender and it is a good idea always to take a bottle with you on holiday as it may alleviate a whole variety of problems – burns, scalds, cuts and sunburn. It can also help with sleeplessness and minor headaches. (See also the First Aid Starter Pack on page 17.)

Burns and Scalds

Depending on the size of the affected area, dab on neat lavender, tea tree or eucalyptus oil on a cotton bud: or submerge the area in cold water to which 10 drops of one of the above oils has been added; or apply a compress with one of these oils. *Serious burns or scalds must be treated by a doctor.*

Toothache

A drop of clove oil on a cotton bud can be applied directly to the tooth and usually brings fairly rapid relief.

Peppermint oil can also give some relief. Neither, however, is a cure so you should visit your dentist as soon as possible.

Peppermint

Insect and Nettle Stings

If an insect sting has been left behind, remove it with tweezers. Then apply 1 drop of neat tea tree or lavender oil on a cotton bud. You can repeat this process (alternating the oils or mixing them together) until you can see or feel an improvement. *If you are allergic to insect stings, and an increasing number of people seem to be, see a doctor immediately.*

Remove the insect sting with tweezers, if necessary, and dab on neat tea tree or lavender oil.

Wounds, Cuts and Grazes

For minor wounds, cuts and grazes, you can apply neat lavender or tea tree oil. They can also be applied as compresses or added to a bath.

Always use a very high protection suncream when sunbathing and cover up sensitive areas like the face and the shoulders at the first sign of trouble. If you get sunburnt, a soak in a lavender or peppermint bath will bring some relief.

Sunburn

If the area is not too inflamed, you can dab on neat lavender oil. For a larger, more sensitive area, add lavender or peppermint oil to a tepid bath and soak in it for at least 20 minutes.

Sprains

If in doubt about any sort of injury, consult a doctor or the accident department in a hospital. If you know it is only a minor sprain or as an interim measure, apply a cold compress using a bowl of water with 3 drops each of eucalyptus, lavender and rosemary oils added. Replace as the compress warms up.

Bruises

For a minor bruise, apply repeated compresses with a flannel soaked in a bowl of water to which 4 drops each of fennel and marjoram oils have been added. Arnica ointment, available from health shops, is also excellent for bruises and, if applied immediately, it can sometimes stop them appearing altogether. Arnica is also available in pill form.

Consulting an Aromatherapist

If you decide to consult an aromatherapist, you must always be sure to find one who is professionally qualified (see opposite). It is also a good idea, if possible, to have a personal recommendation from someone whose opinion you trust. This way, you will also know what to expect when you go for a consultation, as different therapists use different techniques. The most important priority, though, is that there is a feeling of empathy between you and your therapist. If you feel uncomfortable in any way, then this is not the therapist for you.

A professional aromatherapist is particularly useful if you have a specific condition that you feel needs qualified help or if you want a course of treatment – particularly for massage. One of the key areas for aromatherapists is stress, and the very relaxing treatment of a massage with the right essential oils can be of enormous benefit in stress-related problems.

For a first appointment allow between 1½ and 2 hours. Subsequently, the sessions will probably drop to just 1 hour but the first time, the therapist may want to discuss your physical and emotional health in some depth.

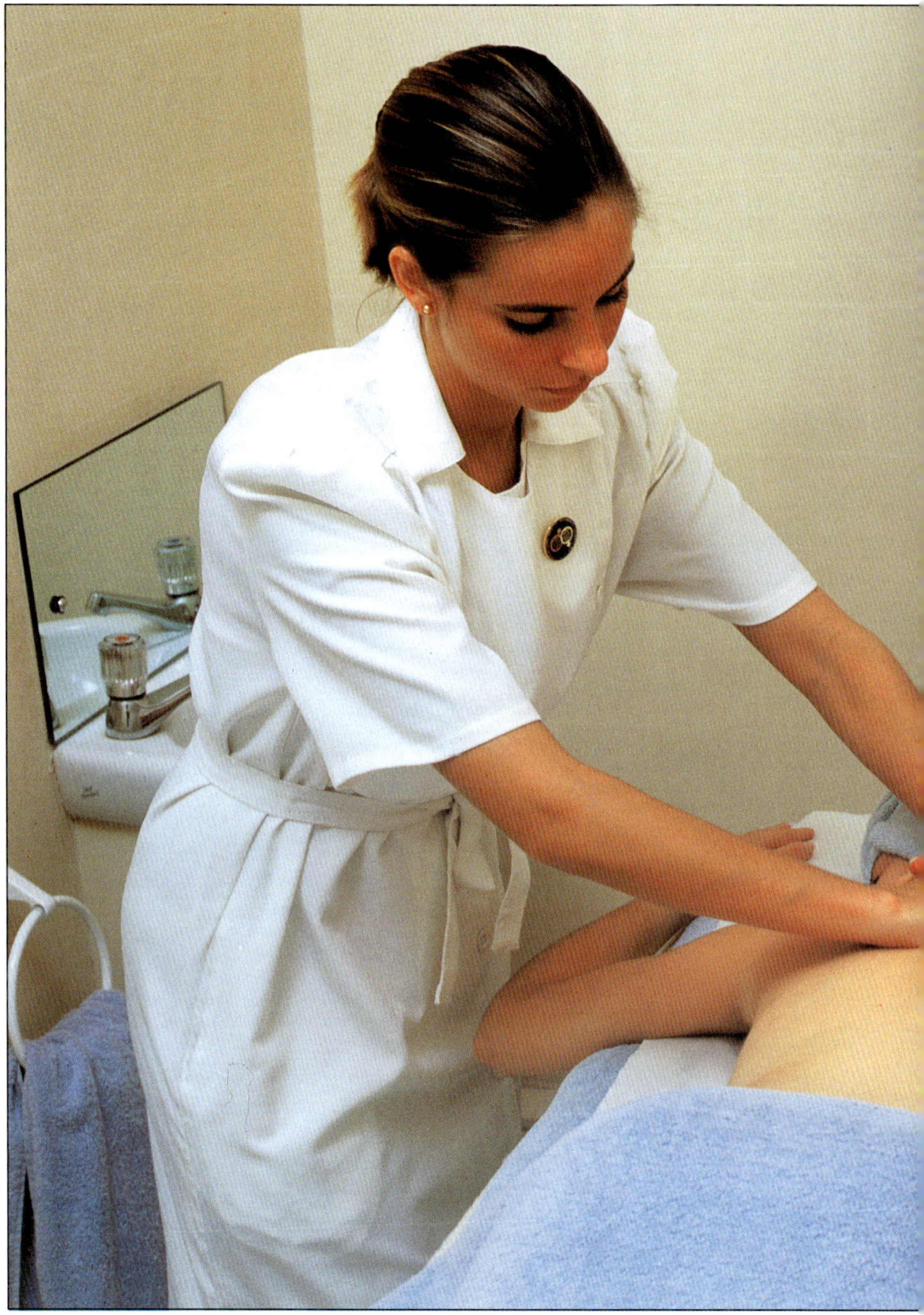

A professional massage from a qualified aromatherapist is a real treat, particularly if you are suffering from stress or any related problems.

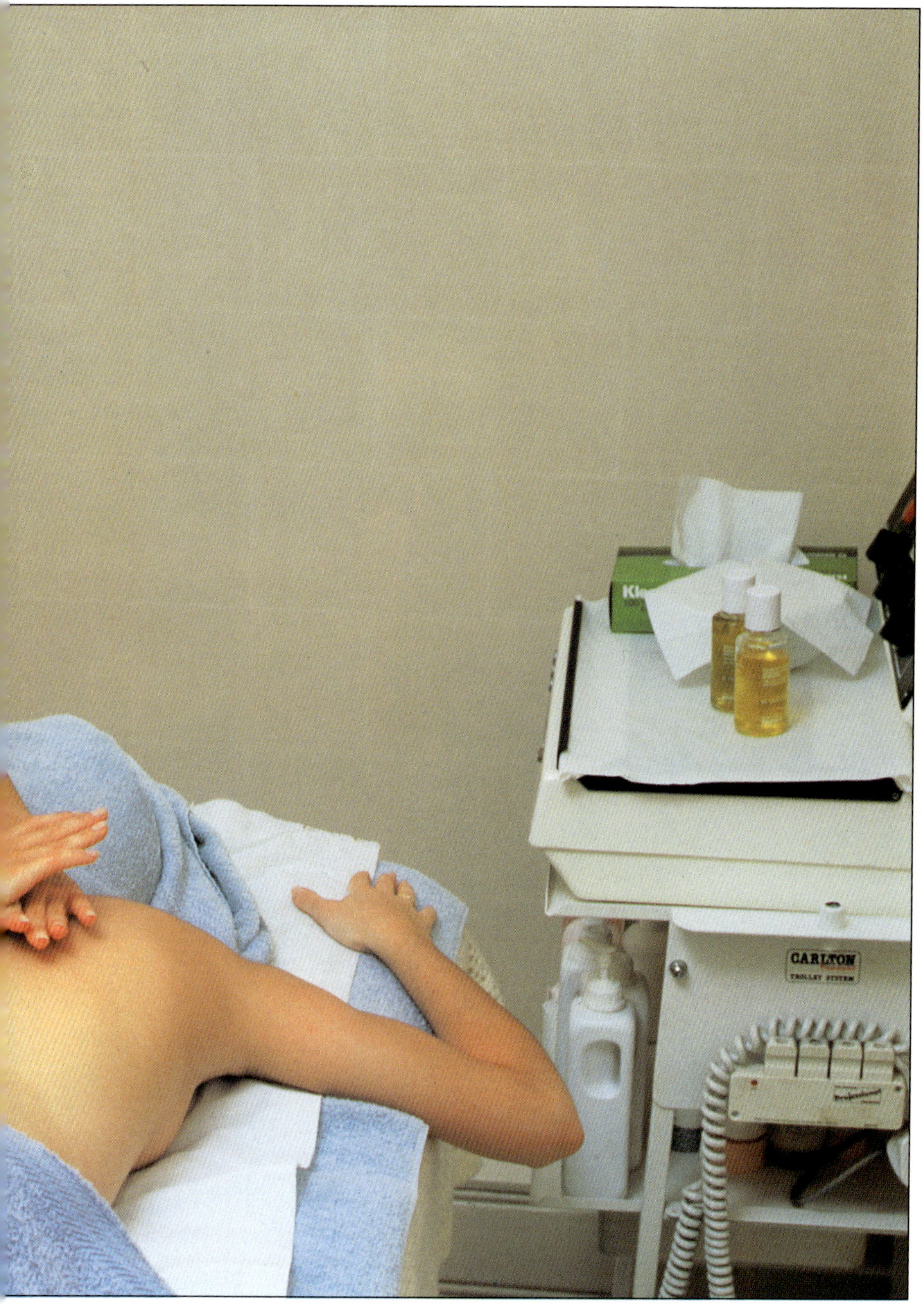

Useful Adresses

Professional associations –
International Federation of
Aromatherapists (IFA)
Stamford House
2–4 Chiswick High Road
London W4 1TH

For a list of qualified practising aromatherapists, send £2 in stamps and a self-addressed envelope

Aromatherapy training courses –
Tisserand Institute
65 Church Road, Hove
East Sussex BN3 2BD
Tel: 01723 206640

Shirley Price Aromatherapy
Wesley House, Stockwell Head
Hinckley, Leicestershire, LE10 1RD
Tel: 01455 615466

Mail order essential oils –
Robert Tisserand
Newtown Road, Hove,
East Sussex BN3 7BA
Tel: 01273 325666

Shirley Price (address as above)

Neal's Yard Apothecary
2 Neal's Yard, Covent Garden
London WC2H 9DP
Tel: 020 7379 7222
(mail order and shop)

Reading List

Shirley Price, *Practical Aromatherapy*
Thorsons, 1983
Maggie Tisserand,
Aromatherapy for Women
Thorsons, 1983
Robert Tisserand,
The Art of Aromatherapy
Daniel, 1977
Dr Jean Valnet,
The Practice of Aromatherapy
Daniel, 1982

HERBAL REMEDIES

TAMARA KIRCHER and PENNY LOWERY

INTRODUCTION

Flowering plants first grew on this planet about 135 million years ago, rapidly evolving into the main groups of plants we recognize today as a result of their differing environments. Farmers who work with traditional methods say that animals know instinctively which plants will be good for them when they are sick; whether this was also the case for the predecessors of the human race, or whether they used trial and error to ascertain which plants did them good and which were harmful or even fatal, there is no way of knowing. Inevitably, though, humans have always had a close relationship with plants, using them as they evolved for food, clothing, rope, shelter, medicine and to feed domestic animals.

Traditionally, the herb garden with its roots, leaves, flowers, and berries provided inspiration for health and wellbeing.

It is thought that the earliest written record of the medicinal use of plants dates back to the Sumerians who described the use and actions of thyme, among other remedies, over 5,000 years ago. The earliest known Chinese herbal, compiled in 2700 BC, lists 365 medicinal substances and their actions; many of these are still in use today, notably Ma Huang (*Ephedra sinica*) from which the modern drug ephedrine is derived. Even Psalms in the Old Testament has some herbal knowledge to impart: "Purge me with Hyssop, and I shall be clean." The Egyptians of 1000 BC are said to have used coriander, mint, garlic and other plants for food, dyes and medicines; and some fundamental principles of healing were expressed by the Greek and Roman medical writers. Hippocrates recommended fresh air, rest and improved diet combined with herbal remedies to restore health, whereas Galen saw the remedies he proposed as a complete system: he included not just plants but medicines derived from animal and mineral sources, as does the classical system of homeopathy. These early Greek writers describe herbal medicines supporting the person's "life force". This concept is similar to the ancient Chinese concept of *Qi* or *Ch'i*, terms which usually mean "energy" but can also mean "air" or "breath". *Qi* is an essential element of Chinese medicinal theory defining the difference between life and inertia or death. The Greek idea of life force also corresponds to *Ki* in Japan, which means the vital force flowing through the body.

The more formal herb garden offers peace and tranquillity through the beauty of its scents, colours and design.

At times in the past, magical properties have been attributed to herbs and those who knew about them; this naturally gave rise to superstition, fear and suspicion, and ultimately the persecution and death of many wise women, healers and witches. Of course some ancient uses of herbs sound like nonsense to us today, and perhaps some of them were completely ineffective: Avicenna, an Italian philosopher of the Middle Ages, recommended a method of contraception in which the woman would drink large quantities of infused basil – *not* to be tried! It was generally believed, in the same historical period, that the root of the mandrake plant shrieked when it was pulled out of the earth, causing insanity followed by death to anyone who heard it. The plant was considered valuable as an anaesthetic and expectorant however; so the bizarre practice evolved of tying a dog to the stem to unearth it!

Not all medieval herbal practices by any means were ineffectual; early surgeons used a sponge soaked in opium, henbane, hemlock, mandrake and ivy which was held close to the patient's nose to inhale, thus deadening the pain of amputation or surgery very effectively. Of course, these herbs are all highly toxic, which meant that if the unfortunate patient breathed the cocktail in too vigorously, he or she was likely to overdose and expire.

Garden thyme, derived from the Greek word "thymus", meaning courage, was used in medieval times to invigorate and to inspire strength and bravery.

Many important herbs, such as echinacea and false unicorn root were part of the extensive herbal tradition of the Native Americans.

HERBS AND THE ENVIRONMENT

Even though little written herbal lore has been inherited from the Native Americans, their use of herbs for healing and rituals is well known through oral records. The discovery of many important herbs like echinacea is thanks to them. Native Americans emphasize the need for people to live in harmony with their surroundings. It has long been the tradition of many tribes, when they take something from the Earth, to compensate by giving something back to her. If all cultures had this principle, our planet might not be threatened by deforestation, intensive farming and over-industrialization. Perhaps because of their all-important relationship with "Grandmother Earth", Native Americans have given us knowledge of, and access to, some particularly valuable herbs for the reproductive system; for example, false unicorn root, which is mentioned in the section on reproduction and urinary problems (see page 102).

Users of herbs are fortunate today: not only do they inherit the wisdom of many cultures to provide them with knowledge about the historical use of plants, but also laboratory investigations have been able to isolate the multitude of chemicals which occur naturally in herbs, enabling people to know what they are good for and why. Some of these constituents are necessary to the life of the plant; a great many, however, are not, which suggests that these natural medicinal substances have been provided for human beings by the planet, to help to sustain life and health. There has probably been more continuity in the use of herbs as medicine than in any other method.

The range of herbs that is now available, with the help of modern infrastructure, is quite extraordinary. Herbs that grow in China and Japan, Europe, Africa and the Americas can be obtained in other countries; whereas our forebears were limited to those that grew in their own neighbourhood. Ironically, intensive farming methods have reduced the availability of herbs that grow wild in the countryside – frequently they are seen as weeds and destroyed in favour of crops. Furthermore, many people live in cities without access to gardens. This need not be an obstacle, however, with commercial sources of herbs, and even mail order, becoming more accessible to everyone.

Until very recently, the manufactured drugs prescribed by doctors were all derived from plants: aspirin from willow and meadowsweet (whose botanical name, *Spirea*, it has borrowed), steroids from wild yam, ephedrine from *Ma Huang*. Some drugs are still synthesized from herbs. This fact may be what saves some parts of our environment; pharmaceutical companies have been known to buy areas of land to prevent its destruction by loggers, as has happened in part of the Brazilian rain forest, so as to ensure that specific plants with medicinal ingredients will still be available. The result of extracting one or two active constituents from a plant, however, is to produce a drug with an isolated action, thus losing the balanced energy of the herb, which originally had many actions that worked holistically on the human organism. Another result of producing chemical drugs in a laboratory is the associated pollution of the environment by toxic waste products; using herbs medicinally has no such negative implications – it means working *with* the environment, not against it.

Herbs and Lifestyle

Herbs are very effective as a way of caring for both our bodies and our psyches, but they will work best if you look after yourself on other levels too: if you eat well, exercise gently but regularly, try to breathe fresh air (when available!) and find ways of dealing with stress, the herbs will have a more harmonious environment with which to work. Although herbs can help with some emotional problems, anyone who is very anxious or distressed, or has unresolved issues from the past, is advised to seek counselling or psychotherapy.

Many herbs are also eaten, either as flavouring or as an intrinsic part of a dish: garlic, fennel, ginger, parsley,

Borage
(Borago officinalis)

thyme, sage and basil are good examples. Some herbals also list foods such as lemon, onions and leeks, and specify their medicinal actions; and extract of lettuce is included in some nervine relaxants for its sedative properties.

It is possible to see food and herbs as part of a continuum, with food that has no medicinal action at one end, moving through the area where herbs and nourishment combine (including culinary herbs and medicinal food), to plants which are only used medicinally. At the extreme end of this continuum there are the herbs which are actually toxic when taken in large amounts, but in smaller quantities may be healing for tumours and other serious conditions, which are of course beyond the scope of this book.

It has been said that being a good herbalist is very similar to being a good cook; prescriptions are just another kind of recipe! Of course, not all herbal mixtures taste good, but everyone knows that good food can benefit our health.

KEY HERBS

There are probably over 2,000 medicinal plants available worldwide – an overwhelming number for the novice herbal user to grapple with! So here is a manageable quantity of herbs which are commonly used, easily available, and safe for most occasions. There is no need to buy all of them at once; you will build up a stock gradually, as you need the different herbs. Remember both tinctures and dried herbs keep best when stored in a cool, dry, dark place. In many cases fresh herbs can be used, if they are available; you will need to use slightly more by weight, to allow for their higher moisture content.

As we mention in the section on *Basic Principles*, it is usual to mix several herbs together, which gives a broader range of actions than using just one herb. So far as we know, all herbs are compatible with each other, and mixing them together can only enhance their healing properties. The table of recommended dosages on page 81 will apply whether you are taking one herb or several, and tinctures mixed together will keep just as long as single tinctures, provided you protect them from sunlight.

In this section, we have given a brief description of the medicinal actions of each herb, the part which is used, and some examples of ailments it is used to treat. We suggest that, when you have found a herb or combination of herbs in the *Specific Applications* section, you cross-check their description here to ensure they are suitable.

Echinacea

(*Echinacea angustifolia*)
Also known as purple cone-flower, Kansas snakeroot, comb flower, black Susan, hedgehog and Sampson root, its botanical name comes from the Greek *echinos*, meaning hedgehog which its flowers resemble. The Native Americans have employed this extremely useful herb for generations to help clear microbial infections, both bacterial and viral, and boost the immune system. It is widely used and combines well with many other herbs, being effective for respiratory tract infections, cystitis, catarrhal conditions, acne, and infected cuts or wounds. It has a reputation as a natural antibiotic, with none of the unfortunate side-effects of antibiotic drugs; historically, it has also been used to treat rattlesnake bite.
PART USED: root

Nettle

(*Urtica dioica*)
This is the common stinging nettle, which grows wild all over the world. It has a wide variety of uses, but is of particular benefit to the urinary system, reproductive organs and skin. It is used against haemorrhage and eczema, and a decoction of the root applied locally to the scalp is said to reduce hair loss!
PART USED: whole plant (collected while in flower)

Cleavers

(*Galium aparine*)

Also known as goosegrass, clivers, hayriffe, burweed or goosebill, cleavers is an excellent tonic for the lymphatic system, and so is used for swollen glands, tonsillitis and glandular fever (often combined with such herbs as poke root and marigold).

It also benefits the skin, has a long history of use for tumours and ulcers, and may be helpful for painful urinary infections like cystitis.

PART USED: whole plant above ground (gathered before pale green flowers are produced in June and July)

Roman chamomile

(*Anthemis nobilis*)

and **German chamomile**

(*Matricaria chamomilla*)

The actions of both varieties are similar. The name chamomile comes from the Greek word which means "ground apple". It is an excellent mild sedative (suitable for use with children) and reduces inflammation

and muscle spasm, such as menstrual cramps. It also aids digestion and reduces flatulence. Used externally, it helps in the healing of wounds, and can also be used as a mouthwash for ulcers or gingivitis.

PART USED: flowers (gathered in summer in dry conditions)

Lavender

(*Lavandula officinalis*)

This common herb has a variety of uses, based on its cooling and sedative properties: it can be effective for headaches, especially those caused by stress, and is often used in combination with other herbs to deal with depression, nervous exhaustion, and other emotional symptoms. It may aid restful sleep, either taken at bedtime as an infusion or slipped under the pillow in a muslin bag. It is sometimes used for rheumatic pain, especially if this is accompanied by inflammation, and skin rashes.

PART USED: flowers (gathered just before they open)

Ginseng

(*Radix ginseng*)

Also known by its Chinese name *Ren Shen*, there are many types of ginseng, each having its own specific properties (sweet, slightly bitter, slightly warm), though all are very strengthening. American ginseng, for example, is cooler in action than Chinese ginseng, and therefore more appropriate for use after high fevers. Ginseng is one of the most widely known and valued Chinese herbs (and one of the most expensive!). Traditionally, it has a reputation for increasing fertility and longevity. It is useful in any condition where there is weakness or exhaustion. In cases of extreme collapse – say, after a serious loss of blood – up to 30g of ginseng can be decocted and drunk. More commonly it is used to benefit a weak digestion or aid recovery after a long illness. It also has a calming quality and can be used short-term for palpitations, insomnia and restlessness accompanied by general debility. *Avoid use in pregnancy, high blood pressure or where there is no weakness.*

PART USED: root

DOSAGE: 1–9g per day

Marigold

(*Calendula officinalis*)

This herb is excellent for external application wherever there are skin rashes, inflammation or lesions; it speeds the healing process and helps prevent infection of cuts, grazes and fungal infections. Compresses or poultices work well, and it is also available in homeopathic potency as *Calendula* ointment. Used internally, marigold aids digestion and benefits the gallbladder. It is also a valuable herb for the reproductive system, easing period pains and regulating the menstrual cycle.

PART USED: flowers or petals (collected in summer)

Astragalus

(Radix astragali membranaceus)

Also known as milk vetch root and by its Chinese name *Huang Qi*, this herb has sweet, slightly warm properties. It is used to strengthen the body, so it helps with fatigue, lack of appetite and diarrhoea. It has the function of "raising the yang *Qi*", so it is useful for prolapses of the uterus, stomach or rectum. According to Chinese medicine, this drug also "stabilizes the protective *Qi*" and helps strengthen the immune system to guard against frequent colds and illnesses. Today it is used in the treatment of AIDS.

PART USED: root (harvested in spring and autumn)

DOSAGE: 9–30g per day

Lemon balm *(below)*

(Melissa officinalis)

Also known as balm mint, bee balm, dropsy plant, garden balm, melissa, or sweet balm, this perennial plant is common both wild and cultivated in Europe and parts of the US. It is a useful digestive herb, relieving spasm in the intestines and flatulence, and because it also has mild sedative properties, it is helpful for anyone whose digestive problems are associated with anxiety or stress. It benefits the heart and lowers both fever and blood pressure.

PARTS USED: aerial parts (either fresh or dried in the shade)

Elecampane

(Inula helenium)

The common name of this herb is said to be a distortion of its Latin title; it is also known as elfwort, scabwort, elfdock, or horseheal. While it is generally cultivated in Britain, the plant grows wild in parts of North America. It soothes coughs, clears catarrh and has an anti-bacterial action, making it effective for asthma, bronchitis, chest infections or even emphysema. It has a history of use in tuberculosis, and is good for coughs in children, often combined with such herbs as hyssop and coltsfoot.

PART USED: rhizome (dug up in the autumn)

Comfrey

(Symphytum officinale)

Also known as knitbone (or nipbone) because of its healing properties in case of fractures, this herb has a long history of external use too as a poultice or compress to speed the healing of wounds and lesions. It also works well internally for stomach ulcers, and may be beneficial for respiratory infections. *Avoid long-term use.*

PARTS USED: root, rhizome and leaves

Chinese angelica *(right)*

(Radix angelicae sinensis)

Also known by its Chinese names *Dang Gui* and *Tang Kuei*, this beautiful herb with its sweet, acrid, bitter and warm properties helps to nourish and move the blood, so it is used after childbirth or blood loss, and for anaemia and menstrual problems. It is warming, so is helpful in relieving pain that is worse with cold, such as some menstrual cramps and hernia pain. It also moves the bowels so it is used to treat constipation with dry stools. *Avoid use with diarrhoea, bloating and cases where there are signs of heat* (flushed face, extreme thirst, etc.)

PART USED: root (harvested in autumn)

DOSAGE: 3–15g per day

Passion-flower
(*Passiflora incarnata*)
Also known as maypops or passion vine, this herb is an excellent sedative and aids restful sleep when taken at night. It is also good for the nerves, and so is used for neuralgia and herpes zoster (shingles). Since it releases muscular tension, it may be useful for asthma or any condition where the muscles are in spasm.
PART USED: dried leaves (collected before flowering)

Golden seal *(above)*
(*Hydrastis canadensis*)
Also known as eye root, eye balm, ground raspberry, and yellowroot, this plant is a native of North America and is also a popular herb in Caribbean cultures. It is a powerful tonic to the mucous membranes, resolves phlegm, and is beneficial to some digestive disorders including loss of appetite. It is invaluable in clearing infections of the upper respiratory tract, but its prolonged use is not advisable as it is very drying. For this reason it is often added to a prescription in half quantities. *It must be avoided in pregnancy*, but can be useful during labour as it stimulates the uterine muscles.
PARTS USED: root and rhizome (unearthed in the autumn)

Licorice *(below)*
(*Glycyrrhiza glabra*)
Also known as sweet wood, this plant, which features in both Western and Chinese herbalism, benefits the endocrine system and is therefore helpful in any illness involving the adrenal glands. For home use, its application is more likely to be for respiratory problems such as bronchitis, or digestive disorders, including ulcers, gastritis and colic.
PART USED: dried root (unearthed in late autumn)

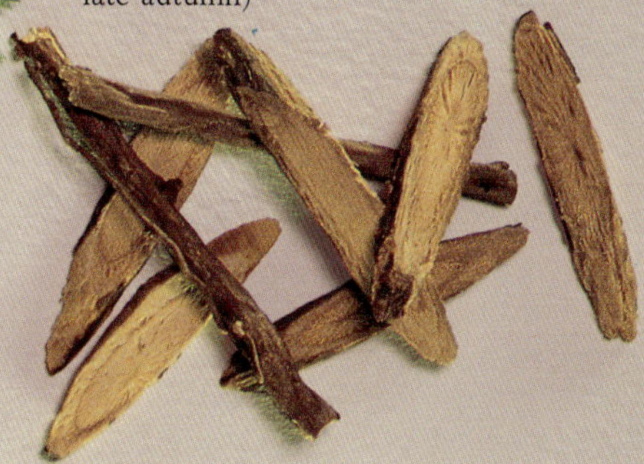

Yarrow
(*Achillea millefolium*)
Also known as milfoil, nosebleed and thousand-leaf, this plant was given its Latin name by botanists on the basis that it would have healed the wounds of Achilles, had he had access to it! This is of course rather fanciful, but this herb *does* have a valuable action on wounds, as the Native Americans have known for many years, using it externally as a powder on wounds and sores, or infused to treat burns, fevers and colds. They also burn it: the smoke forms an incense to ward off negative energies. Yarrow is found in the USA and in Europe; the American variety is said to be stronger. When taken, it promotes sweating and so helps the body through feverish illness; it clears heat from the urinary tract, and so has a role in cystitis; and it is also said to lower blood pressure.
PART USED: whole plant above ground (collected when in flower)

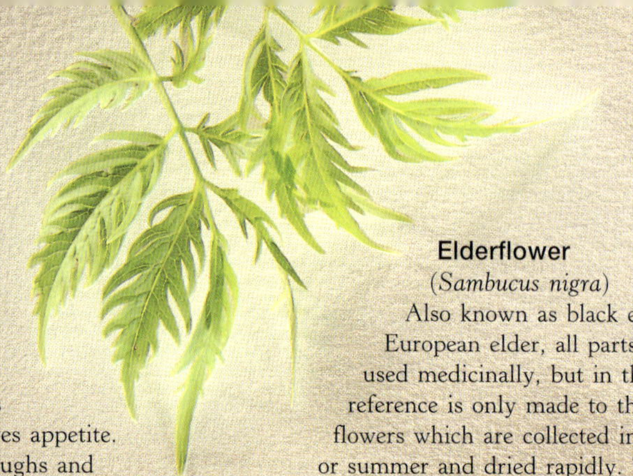

Fennel *(left)*

(Foeniculum vulgare)

Fennel, which appears in both Chinese and Western herbs, relieves flatulence, is good for colic, and improves appetite. It also is said to relieve coughs and improve the flow of milk in women who are breast-feeding. Used externally, as a compress, it relieves inflammation of the eyes (try combining it with eyebright). In both China and the Western world, it is used as a food; but in China it is also regarded as aiding the digestion and helping pain from hernia.

PART USED: seeds

Thyme

(Thymus vulgaris)

Like sage, thyme is a common garden shrub, though it can grow wild; also like sage, it is used for culinary purposes. It does have a broad range of medicinal applications, too – it soothes coughs and sore throats, aids digestion, reduces gas, combats infection, and is mildly astringent so helps in diarrhoea and incontinence, especially in children. It is also used for a range of respiratory problems including whooping cough and bronchitis.

PARTS USED: leaves and flowers (collected in summer)

Elderflower

(Sambucus nigra)

Also known as black elder or European elder, all parts can be used medicinally, but in this book reference is only made to the flowers which are collected in spring or summer and dried rapidly. They are useful in the treatment of colds and flu, as they clear catarrh and induce sweating. Hay fever and sinusitis also respond well, and deafness following a cold (usually due to mucus in the Eustachian tubes) may be treated with this herb.

PARTS USED: see above

Dandelion

(Taraxacum officinale)

The name of this common weed is said to come from the French *dents de lion*, meaning lion's teeth – a reflection on the shape of its leaves. It is an excellent diuretic, and a good source of potassium, an essential mineral usually lost from the body when synthetic diuretics are taken. It has a cleansing effect on the liver and gallbladder, so is used in cases of jaundice and indigestion (especially when constipation is involved).

PART USED: root (collected between June and August) or leaves

Valerian *(above)*

(Valeriana officnalis)

Also called Capon's tail, this herb is an outstanding nervine relaxant, combining well with other herbs such as hops and passion-flower to deal with insomnia in adults. It also reduces muscle cramp and is therefore effective against pain caused by spasm, such as colic or menstrual cramps. It is an excellent sedative, and may be used instead of chemical tranquillizers if the patient is tense, anxious or panicky. It is not recommended for long-term use however; after taking it for about six weeks, have a three-week break before using it again.

PARTS USED: root and rhizome (unearthed in autumn)

Coltsfoot *(above)*
(*Tussilago farfara*)
Also known as coughwort, horsehoof, British tobacco, butterbur or foal's-foot, this herb with its hoof-shaped leaves has a legendary effect on coughs and most other respiratory problems, including asthma, bronchitis, emphysema and whooping cough. It is soothing, anti-spasmodic and expectorant, and combines well with hyssop, elecampane, lobelia and other herbs which benefit the lungs.
PARTS USED: leaves (gathered in May or June) and flowers (usually collected in March or April before they have fully bloomed)

Chrysanthemum flower
(*Chrysanthemi morifolium*)
Also known by its Chinese name *Ju Hua*, this flower has sweet, bitter and slightly cold properties. It is most commonly used for clearing colds accompanied by fever and headache. It can also be used on its own to help strengthen the eyes, for conditions such as red, painful, and dry eyes, blurred vision and spots in front of the eyes. It has a calming effect and can help with dizziness and headaches caused by tension.
PART USED: flowers (harvested in full bloom)
DOSAGE: 4–15g per day

Vervain
(*Verbena officinalis*)
This herb is an excellent mild sedative, which strengthens the nervous system while also having a calming effect. It is available in tea-bags in parts of Europe, and makes a pleasant bedtime drink. This herb also helps deal with depression, especially if this is caused by the depletion of energy after a virus, and is often most effective combined with oats and skullcap. It benefits the liver and gallbladder, (organs which Chinese medicine see as playing a role in depression), and so may be of help in jaundice and hepatitis.
PART USED: whole plant above ground (collected in July just before blooming)

Sage
(*Salvia officinalis*)
Also known as red sage or garden sage, this herb has a specific action on the mouth and throat, and will benefit most conditions in that area, especially where there is inflammation. It is often used as a mouthwash or gargle, and will benefit sore throats, mouth ulcers, bleeding gums, tonsillitis and laryngitis. It will also work for these conditions when taken internally, and its other actions include reducing flatulence, slowing the production of breast milk, and inducing sweating. It has another use in the Native American tradition: the dried leaves are burned and the smoke is used as incense for cleansing negative energies – white mountain sage is preferred for this use. *It should be avoided in pregnancy.*
PART USED: leaves (collected in May or June, and dried in the shade)

Other Herbs

This section briefly describes all the remaining herbs mentioned in the *Ailments* section, so that you can check their suitability before taking or prescribing them. Many herbals list a thousand herbs or more; this book includes only about a hundred, which may still sound a lot if you are new to the subject! There is no need to attempt to familiarize yourself with all of them; in time you will get to know the ones you use often. Here we have simply listed each herb's common name, Latin name and main actions.

Borage
(*Borago officinalis*)

Agnus castus berries (*Vitex agnus-castus*)
Also called chaste tree; tonic and normalizer for the female reproductive system.

Agrimony (*Agrimonia eupatoria*)
Has an astringent action on the digestive tract; specific for diarrhoea in children.

Barley grain (*Hordeum vulgare*)
Cooling and moist, benefiting the stomach, throat and bladder; commonly used for cystitis.

Basil (*Ocimum basilicum*)
Used against stomach cramps, vomiting, constipation and gastro-enteritis.

Bayberry (*Myrica cerifera*)
A circulatory stimulant; valuable in diarrhoea, colitis, sore throats and colds.

Black cohosh (*Cimicifuga racemosa*)
Native American herb, excellent to relax and normalize the reproductive system.

Blackcurrant leaves (*Ribes nigrum*)
Cool and drying action; helpful to the digestive and urinary systems.

Blue cohosh (*Caulophyllum thalictroides*)
Also called squaw root and papoose root, uterine tonic; helps delayed menses or labour pains.

Boneset (*Eupatorium perfoliatum*)
Excellent remedy for flu, colds and fevers.

Borage leaves (*Borago officinalis*)
Benefit the adrenal gland; help in stress, fevers and convalescence.

Buchu (*Agathosma betulina*)
Diuretic, very useful for urinary infections or whenever there is pain or discomfort on urination.

Burdock root (*Arctium lappa*)
Valuable for dry skin conditions, rheumatism, kidney problems and wounds.

Caraway seeds (*Carum carvil*)
Benefit the digestion, helping flatulence and colic and loss of appetite or diarrhoea.

Cardamom (*Elettaria cardamomum*)
Reduces wind and griping pains; improves appetite and flow of saliva.

Catnip (*Nepeta cataria*)
Eases stomach upsets involving flatulence; also good for colds and flu.

Cayenne (*Capsicum minimum*)
Stimulant to the digestive and circulatory systems; antiseptic.

Celery seeds (*Apium graveolens*)
Diuretic with specific action on arthritis, rheumatism and other joint pains.

Chickweed (*Stellaria media*)
Cool moist herb used externally for wounds or rashes, internally for rheumatism.

Cinnamon (*Cinnamomum zeylanicum*)
Helps against wind, nausea, vomiting and diarrhoea.

Cloves (*Eugenia caryophyllus*)
Stimulates digestion, alleviates nausea, vomiting and flatulence; antiseptic and anaesthetic properties make it useful locally, eg for toothache.

Cornsilk *(Zea mays)*
Cool moist herb which soothes any inflammation of the urinary tract.

Couchgrass *(Agropyron repens)*
Also benefits the urinary system; used for cystitis, urethritis, prostatitis and kidney stones.

Crampbark *(Vinurnum opulus)*
Named after its action, relaxes muscle tension anywhere in the body; may prevent threatened miscarriage.

Damiana *(Turnera aphrodisiaca)*
Tonic for hormonal and nervous systems, and anti-depressant.

Eyebright *(Euphrasia officinalis)*
As its name suggests, reduces inflammation in the eyes; also benefits the mucous membranes and clears catarrh.

False unicorn root
(Chamaelirium luteum)
Tonic for both male and female reproductive systems; used in ovarian pain, threatened miscarriage, and late or absent menstruation.

Feverfew *(Tanacetum parthenium)*
Relieves migraines and headaches, "hot" arthritis, dizziness, tinnitus, and painful or hesitant menstrual flow.

Forsythia *(Forsythia)*
Also known by its Chinese name *Lian Qiao*. Expels "wind-heat", ie sudden onset of feverish virus; therefore used at first sign of cold or flu.

Ginger *(Zingiber officinale)*
Stimulates the circulation, induces sweating, settles flatulence, and relieves sore throats.

Hawthorn berries
(Crataegus oxyacanthoides)
Normalize the activity of the heart, and are therefore useful in palpitations and high blood pressure.

Honeysuckle *(Lonicera)*
Also known by its Chinese name *Jin Yin Hua*. Often used in combination with forsythia in a slightly higher dosage (9–15g, daily) for feverish colds and flu.

Hops *(Humulus lupulus)*
Sedative herb, relieving anxiety, insomnia, and nervous diarrhoea or indigestion. *Avoid long-term use; do not prescribe if patient is depressed.*

Hyssop *(Hyssopus officinalis)*
Excellent to soothe coughs, induce sweating, and calm anxiety states.

Jamaican dogwood
(Piscidia erythrina)
Acts as a pain reliever and sedative; particularly useful if there is insomnia as a result of pain.

Lime blossom *(Tilia europea)*
A relaxant herb which lowers blood pressure; also used against migraines and colds.

Longan fruit
Also known by its Chinese name *Long Yan Rou*. Nourishes the blood and calms the spirit; used for insomnia, forgetfulness, palpitations and dizziness.

Marjoram *(Origanum vulgare)*
This culinary herb has a valuable action in colds, coughs and flu, as it induces sweating and has antiseptic properties.

Marshmallow *(Althaea officinalis)*
Both root and leaf are cool and moist; the root acts on the digestion and skin, the leaf on the lungs and urinary system.

Meadowsweet *(Filipendula ulmaria)*
Excellent digestive remedy; used to treat childhood diarrhoea and also rheumatism.

Motherwort *(Leonurus cardiaca)*
Benefits circulation, therefore useful in heart conditions and to regularize menstruation; often used in menopause.

Mullein *(Verbascum thapsus)*
Has an anti-inflammatory effect on the lungs, and so soothes coughs. The oil is used to soften ear wax.

Oats *(Avena sativa)*
Nourishing to the nervous system; excellent for nervous exhaustion and depression.

Parsley *(Petroselinum crispum)*
Besides being rich in Vitamin C, is a diuretic, can help bring on menstruation, and eases wind. *Avoid large amounts in pregnancy.*

Pasque flower *(Anemone pulsatilla)*
Relieves period pains and tension headaches; also useful for the skin and respiratory system.

Pennyroyal
(Mentha pulegium)
Releases muscle spasms, relieving colicky indigestion. Its main use is to bring on delayed menstruation. *Avoid in pregnancy.*

Peppermint
(*Mentha piperata*)
Rich in volatile oils, is an excellent digestive, relieving flatulence, nausea and morning sickness; also helps reduce feverish colds and flu.

Prickly ash
(*Xanthoxylum americanum*)
Stimulates circulation and lymphatic drainage; used in rheumatism and skin diseases.

Raspberry leaf
(*Rubus idaeus*)
Traditionally used to strengthen and tone the uterine muscles during pregnancy and labour; also valuable for diarrhoea and mouth ulcers.

Red clover
(*Trifolium pratense*)
Most commonly used for skin problems in children; also against coughs.

Rhubarb root (*Rheum palmatum*)
Not the same as garden rhubarb; excellent for constipation and cleansing the intestines.

Roses
(*Rosa gallica*)
Any red rose petals can be used medicinally, usually hybrid perpetuals; also the hips of the dog rose have similar actions: as a tonic or astringent, or to calm the nerves and boost immunity.

Rosemary
(*Rosmarinus officinalis*)
Acts as a stimulant to the circulation and nervous system; helps digestion and muscular pain.

Rue (*Ruta graveolens*)
Regulates menses and eases spasm in the digestive tract.
Avoid in pregnancy.

Saw palmetto (*Serenoa serrulata*)
Strengthens the male reproductive system and is beneficial in prostatitis and urinary infections.

Shepherd's purse
(*Capsella bursa-pastoris*)
Has a mild diuretic action, also regulates menstruation; its astringent effect helps against diarrhoea and bleeding.

Skullcap (*Scutellaria laterifolia*)
Nervine tonic and relaxant: excellent for premenstrual and other tension.

Slippery elm (*Ulmus fulva*)
Has a cool moist action on inflamed or sensitive digestive systems; good during convalescence.

Squaw vine (*Mitchella repens*)
Native American herb, excellent in preparation for childbirth; also helps period pains.

St John's wort (*Hypericum perforatum*)
Sedative and analgesic, therefore useful in many painful conditions; also helps menopausal mood swings.

Tangerine peel
Also known by its Chinese name *Chen Pi*. Benefits digestion, relieves nausea, settles flatulence and bloating.

Tansy (*Tanacetum vulgare*)
Clears intestinal worms from the digestive tract, improves digestion, and brings on menstruation.
Avoid use long-term or in pregnancy.

Wild cherry (*Prunus serotina*)
Soothes the cough reflex, useful in any form of cough.

Wild yam (*Dioscorea villosa*)
Benefits digestion and menstruation; relieves painful, inflamed joints and regulates hormonal function.

Yellow dock (*Rumex crispus*)
Cleanses the blood, good for chronic skin conditions, and eases constipation.

CHINESE HERBAL FORMULAE

These combinations of Chinese herbs are based on well-known traditional herbal prescriptions. They are made into pill form, a more convenient way to take herbs than decoctions which require daily cooking and drinking. They are less potent than decoctions but still very effective.

Western manufacturers are now producing variations on these traditional formulae. Pills or powders may include other herbs which enhance or slightly alter their actions. The brand name will be different, but the name of the traditional formulae on which they are based should be stated.

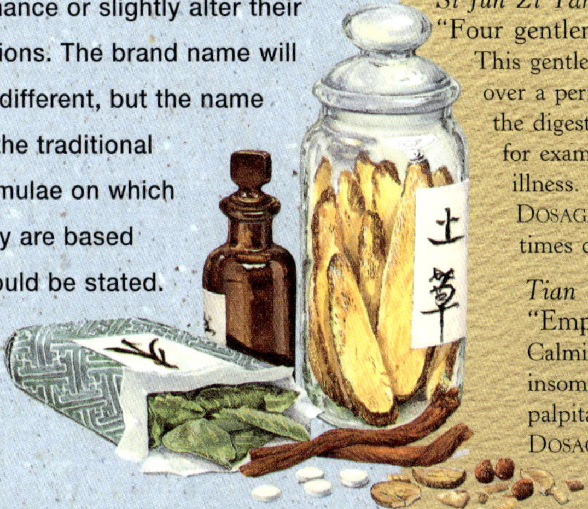

Bi Yan Pian "Clear the nose pill"
Helps clear heat and congestion in hay fever, rhinitis, and sinus problems.
DOSAGE: 4–6 tablets, three times daily.

Dang Gui Bu Xue Tang "Angelica decoction to tonify the blood"
Nourishes the blood and *Qi*; often used after childbirth or with anaemia.
DOSAGE: 5 tablets, two or three times daily.

Nu Ke Ba Zhen Wan
"Women's precious pills"
Very good general tonic for women, especially after childbirth, fatigue, or blood loss.
DOSAGE: 5 tablets, two or three times daily.

Qi Ju Di Huang Wan
Lycium fruit, chrysanthemum and rehmannia pill
This nourishing formula is used for dry or painful eyes with loss of visual acuity, photophobia and tearing when exposed to the wind. Helpful for the elderly.

Shen Ling Bai Zhu Pian
Benefits digestion, especially with loose stools and diarrhoea; good for wind, bloating, indigestion. Safe for children and long-term use.
DOSAGE: 5 tablets, twice daily (halve for children).

Si Jun Zi Tang
"Four gentlemen decoction"
This gentle formula may be taken over a period of time to strengthen the digestion and *Qi* (vital force), for example after a debilitating illness.
DOSAGE: 5 tablets, two or three times daily.

Tian Wang Bu Xin Wan
"Emperor's tea"
Calming formula, used for insomnia, anxiety and palpitations.
DOSAGE: 5 pills, twice daily.

Chinese medicinal herbs are taken as decoctions or ground into pills and powders.

Xiao Yao Wan
"Free and easy wanderer"
Benefits the liver and circulation, thus helping a range of symptoms including digestive and menstrual problems.
DOSAGE: 5 pills, twice daily.

Xiang Sha Liu Jun Wan
"Six gentlemen tea pill"
Strengthens weak digestion; helps with bloating and flatulence.
DOSAGE: 5 pills, twice daily.

Yin Qiao Jie Du Pien
"Dispel heat tablets"
Used immediately at the first sign of a feverish cold or flu, will help sore throats and sometimes prevent the virus developing.
DOSAGE: 5 pills every 2–3 hours on first day, reducing.

Yu Ping Feng San
"Jade windscreen powder"
Used to protect against recurrent colds and strengthen immunity, can be taken over a period of several months.
DOSAGE: 5 tablets, two or three times daily.

BASIC PRINCIPLES

Herbs are available from suppliers in a number of different forms, the main ones being loose dried herbs and tinctures. It is largely a matter of personal preference which one you choose; some people enjoy handling the loose herbs, and consider their texture, appearance and aroma essential to their healing properties. On the other hand, there is no doubt that tinctures (a solution of the herb in alcohol) are more convenient and keep longer. Feel free to experiment until you find the form that suits you. There are a few guidelines however. Some herbs – golden seal, yarrow and valerian, for example – have a taste which most people find unpleasant, and therefore if the prescription you are making up contains one of these, you may find tinctures more palatable; as tinctures are so concentrated, they are taken in smaller quantities. Herbs which consist of the root or bark of the plant, such as echinacea, will need boiling (known as decoction) for the full therapeutic action to be derived.

Because tinctures consist of the herb suspended in an alcoholic base, and the energy of alcohol tends to be heating, some herbalists prefer to avoid tinctures for certain conditions, such as fevers or inflammation. To avoid this problem, take them well-diluted.

It is possible to make your own herbal tea bags from small muslin bags to avoid having to strain an infusion.

PRECAUTIONS

Herbs are generally safe to use for old and young, with very few side effects. However, caution is necessary in some conditions, such as pregnancy. In pregnant women a great deal of energy is being invested in creating new life; this amazing system is a delicate balance which functions best with minimal intervention. There are a number of herbs which can enhance a woman's health in pregnancy; but there are also some which are unsuitable and must be avoided. A full list is given in the section on pregnancy (page 105).

Some sensitive individuals may have an adverse reaction to certain herbs. If this happens, in the form of rashes, headaches, nausea, or any other unfamiliar symptoms, it is advisable to stop taking the herbs and consult a qualified herbalist. People with weak digestion occasionally have difficulty tolerating tinctures; if they upset your stomach, try taking the herbs as an infusion or decoction instead.

CHOOSING THE HERBS

Herbs work holistically; they have a range of actions that work harmoniously together on the human organism, which is one of their advantages over allopathic drugs, which generally have a single, fairly aggressive, action. For this reason, it is usually quite safe to take just one herb. For example, if you are getting flu, you may want to take echinacea; it will support your immune system, help combat the virus, and reduce excessive mucus.

However, it may be helpful to take two or more herbs together to cover a broader range of actions. For example, you may want to combine echinacea with two or three other herbs, such as yarrow to help with a fever; cleavers or marigold for swollen glands; and golden seal to clear the mucous membranes. If you are restless or having difficulty sleeping, you can add a relaxing herb such as skullcap or passion-flower. Most of the herbal prescriptions suggested in this book consist of several herbs which combine well together. You can work out your own prescriptions when you become familiar with the herbs. It is also useful to remember that herbs work on an emotional as well as a physical level; so, if you are choosing a herb for a cough, and the patient is also excitable or insomniac, you may want to choose hyssop which has mild sedative qualities as well as being an expectorant.

The Bach flower remedies are a complete system which uses the healing properties of flowers, prescribed solely according to the patient's emotional state. They are on pages 118-121.

A pot of herbal tea provides a refreshing alternative to black tea or coffee, offering a pleasant drink and a remedy for your ailment.

RECOMMENDED DOSAGES

	ADULTS	CHILDREN AND 70+
INFUSIONS:	*1–2 cups, three times daily*	*½ cup, three times daily*
DECOCTIONS:	*1 cup, two or three times daily*	*½ cup, three times daily*
TINCTURES:	*10 drops – 5ml (1 tbsp), three times daily*	*5–10 drops, three times daily*

The quantities shown in this easy-reference table will be similar whether you are taking a single herb or a mixture. Where a combination of herbs is recommended, it is generally appropriate to mix them in equal quantities. Some herbs may appear in half quantities compared with the other herbs in the prescription; golden seal is one such herb, as it has a slightly aggressive drying action and is best taken in small quantities for short periods of time. However, the above dosages are generally applicable and, where they vary from this, they have been explained elsewhere, such as Chinese herbs where the exact weight in grams should be decocted for longer than usual (45 minutes).

INFUSION

An infusion is like a tea of herb or herbal mixture – in fact, most people use a teapot to prepare their infusions. Infusion is a good method for preparing leaves and flowers, such as marshmallow, lavender or nettles. While most infusions require steeping the leaves in hot water, if your mixture contains any roots or bark, you will have to boil it first.

To make an infusion, put 2 tsp of the herbal mixture in a warmed teapot (a glass or china teapot is best for this, avoid metal if possible) and add two cupfuls of boiling water. Leave to steep for 10–15 minutes, stirring occasionally. It is usual to drink the infusion hot, but there is no reason why you should not take it cold or even iced, if you prefer; if you need to sweeten the tea, use honey, barley malt, apple juice concentrate or liquorice root.

DECOCTION

This means boiling or simmering. It is the method used for any herb which consists of a woody or hard part of the plant: roots, bark, seeds or rhizomes. Add about 30g (1 oz) of the herbal mixture to each 500ml (16 fl oz) of water in a pan. It is best to use one made of glass or ceramic; metal is not ideal, but will suffice – avoid aluminium at all costs, as it is toxic and traces will be transferred to the herbs. Bring to the boil and simmer for 10–15 minutes, then let the mixture cool for a short time and strain it, squeezing the herbs to extract all the beneficial juices.

One disadvantage of decoction is that it may tend to boil off the volatile oils in some plants, thus losing their remedial effect: for example, the volatile oils in fennel, aniseed and peppermint benefit digestion, and so these herbs will not be so effective if boiled. If you have a prescription which contains roots and leaves, you may prefer to prepare them separately and then mix the resulting liquids before drinking them; or, after making the decoction, add the leaves and flowers while the mixture is still hot, and leave the brew to stand for 10 minutes. Alternatively, roots *can* be effectively infused if they are finely powdered beforehand; some herbalists now stock powdered herbs.

Drinking herbal teas regularly over a period of time can enhance health, increase vitality and induce a general feeling of wellbeing.

CHINESE HERBS

Chinese herbs are generally boiled for longer – about 45 minutes is usual. The result is quite dense and may taste unpleasant, but is generally very effective!

Simmer roots, barks and seeds gently for 10–15 minutes to extract their essences and make a beneficial medicinal tea.

Tinctures

This term generally refers to a herbal solution in alcohol; more rarely it can be used for a preparation based in vinegar or glycerine. The advantages of tinctures include their very long shelf life (about two years), convenience, and the fact that alcohol acts as a good solvent for most of the active ingredients of the herb. Tinctures may be somewhat more expensive than loose herbs in their dried form.

It is possible to make tinctures at home, but it is a lengthy process and the result will probably not be as strong or last as well as those bought from a herbal supplier. Such suppliers often sell the tinctures in 500ml (16 fl oz) bottles, which is a fairly large amount for the home user; some will sell them in smaller quantities however, or even mix up a number of herbs in one bottle, if that suits your purpose.

Many people dilute tinctures in half a glass of water or apple juice, though you can dilute them in a cup of tea! Coffee itself has strong actions as a diuretic and stimulant, so it would not serve well as a dilutant. Since alcohol boils off at very low temperatures, an added benefit of the tea is that some of the alcohol in the tincture will evaporate. For children, the dose is shown in the table on page 81. Take at least half an hour before meals.

Tonic Wines

It is also possible to steep herbs in wine to produce your own tonic wines: they are said to taste very pleasant although they will not last as long as a spirit-based tincture. Many aperitifs and liqueurs started out as herbal remedies intended to aid digestion.

Alcohol and vinegar are used to preserve herbs.

Herbal tinctures are easy to take and last for up to two years.

SYRUPS

These may be a useful way to persuade children to take herbs – they are also soothing in the case of coughs. Frequent use is not really recommended because of the harmful effects of too much sugar; you are in danger of cancelling out the benefit of the herbs!

Syrups are simple to make: combine 600ml (1 pt) of boiling water with 900g (2 lb) of sugar in a pan, bring back to the boil, stirring continuously, and immediately turn off the heat. Mix the resulting syrup base with the required tincture/s (three parts syrup to one part tincture) and store in the refrigerator. Syrups also work well used as a gargle.

Coltsfoot syrup helps to soothe and stop coughs.

Children find syrups are a pleasant way of taking herbs.

TABLETS AND POWDERS

Some herbs are readily available in tablet form: echinacea tablets, for example, are often found in wholefood shops, as are a range of herbal sedative tablets, usually combining valerian, passion-flower, hops and extract of lettuce.

Chinese herbal patent formulae – tried and tested prescriptions, some of which have been in use for thousands of years – are also most commonly found in tablet form (see pages 88-9). They are sometimes also available in tincture form.

Powdered herbs are becoming more available, and these can be eaten dry, mixed with water and drunk, or put in gelatine capsules and swallowed. The variety which are freeze-dried from a decoction are best; if they are simply a finely ground version of the dried herb, it is unlikely that the full medicinal value of the herb is obtained.

Passion-flower is a common ingredient of herbal tablets to aid sleep and relaxation.

COMPRESSES AND POULTICES

These are two more methods of applying herbal remedies externally. Compresses consist of any clean cloth or cotton wool soaked in a hot infusion or decoction and applied to the skin, as hot as is comfortable.

Poultices consist of a paste made by mixing the herbs with water; this is then placed between layers of thin cloth such as gauze or muslin. Applied locally, they can speed the healing process in affected areas; herbs such as comfrey or marshmallow are often used.

Compress *– Soak a clean cloth in an appropriate herbal tea. Use to heal external injuries or skin conditions.*

Comfrey poultice *– Leaves are used externally to heal sprains and severe cuts, soothe pain and inflammation, and drain boils and abscesses.*

BATHS

The healing properties of herbs are absorbed very efficiently through the skin, so herbal baths (either the whole body or a foot- or hand-bath) deserve a mention. For a whole body bath, either add about 600ml (1 pt) of a decoction or infusion to the water, or hang the fresh or dried herbs in a muslin bag under the hot tap while running the water.

Foot-baths and hand-baths consist of the undiluted herbal preparation. This is an effective method to induce a good night's sleep; use valerian, skullcap, and hops for adults, or lime blossom and chamomile, which have a gentler action, for children. Similarly, some infusions, when cool, are excellent for local external application: a weak infusion of eyebright, for example, works very well for bathing sore or infected eyes. This method is effective for animals too. (Remember to allow the liquid to cool first!)

Chamomile
(Anthemis nobilis)

Using herbs in baths is a simple way of relaxing.

Yin and Yang

The theory of yin and yang is attributable to early Chinese civilization and its philosophers. It is quite possible to use and prescribe herbs without a thorough understanding of these principles, but it is an important part of Chinese herbal medicine, and has a bearing on the understanding of some Western herbal actions too.

The yin-yang theory postulates the idea that all the systems in the universe consist of these two conflicting yet interdependent energies: from yin and yang originate all the myriad forms of creation. They can be roughly likened to water and fire in their respective natures, but there is a risk of over-simplifying these concepts to make them comprehensible to the Western mind! The following list may give you an idea of the ways in which these two forces exist in contrast to each other:

YIN
Marshmallow leaves
(Althaea officinalis)

YIN (WATER)	YANG (FIRE)
cold	heat
moon	sun
below	above
heavy	light
dim	bright
still	active
being	doing
wet	dry
slow	rapid
night	day

From these comparisons it is hopefully becoming evident that the nature of yang tends to be hot, bright, upward and active; it is often seen as embodying a more masculine energy. Yin, on the other hand, is cool, moist, inward and more nourishing, and is generally seen as being more feminine in its nature. There are no value judgements in this system; each energy provides a perfect complement and antithesis to the other, and cannot exist in isolation.

Ideally, these energies should be in balance in the human body/mind; if they are, good health will prevail. If either energy is depleted, it will affect the other adversely, and illness will eventually be the result. This interdependence is demonstrated sometimes in terms of disease; when suffering from a feverish illness accompanied by a high temperature and sweating, for example, the person feels hot, dry and lacking in energy, and this feeling can sometimes last for a time after the fever has passed. This

YIN
Rose
(Rosa gallica officinalis)

is because the body fluids (yin) have been depleted by the heating effect of the fever. Herbs can help to restore the water/fire balance in the body.

Some herbs are more cool and moist (or yin) in their energy and actions, and they can be used to cool, lubricate and soften the digestive tract or lungs. Examples are marshmallow, coltsfoot and slippery elm. Others are more drying and warming, such as lady's mantle, which is a tonic for the reproductive system, and is more yang in its action. Some herbs are both cooling *and* drying: golden seal and echinacea are good examples, which is why they are so useful for clearing infections in all parts of the body.

In general, the leaves and flowers of a plant are more cooling in action, and its roots more warming, though there are exceptions to this rule. When choosing herbs for a particular individual or symptom, it is helpful to have an awareness of the "temperature" of the herbs you are using, in relation to the energy of the patient. This is particularly true when using Chinese herbs and patent formulae, which can be quite powerful (see page 79).

YANG
Ginger root
(Zingiber officinale)

YANG
Cinnamon
(Cinnamomum zeylanicum)

YANG
Dandelion root
(Taraxacum officinale)

CHINESE HERBAL MEDICINE

Chinese herbal medicine has a rich tradition that dates back to manuscripts from the end of the third century BC found in the Ma Wang Tui tomb in the Hunan province. The Yellow Emperor's Inner Classic, believed to have been compiled about 2,000 years ago, contains many of the theoretical foundations of traditional Chinese medicine. The true originator of Chinese herbal formulae is Zhang Zhong-Jing who wrote his treatise, the *Shang han za bing lun* (Discussion of cold-induced disorders and miscellaneous diseases) at the end of the third century AD. These basic formulae have evolved over the years to play a large part in modern Chinese medicine.

The other major work, the *Wen bing tiao bian* (Systematic differentiation of warm diseases), written in the late eighteenth century by Wu Ju-Tong, provides further insight into the diagnoses and treatments using Chinese herbal formulae. These classical texts have been the basis for much debate that has led to the development of many of the formulae that are used in modern Chinese medicine.

A Chinese herbal prescription can contain a striking variety of herbs.

The properties of Chinese herbs were discovered long before modern scientific methods were developed. Centuries of testing through trial and error as well as the discussions that the many treatises on herbs have engendered have led to well-defined descriptions of the herbs. More recently the herbs have been put through the scrutiny of biochemical analysis. In some cases this has confirmed their traditional uses. In others, researchers have been puzzled as to why certain herbal combinations actually cure disease. New uses have also been discovered for some herbs – for example, some have been found to be anti-carcinogenic.

Traditionally, Chinese herbs have been classified according to the "temperature" they induce, their taste, the "channel" they enter and whether they are yin, yang or neutral. For example, astragalus (*Huang Qi*) is sweet and slightly warming, enters the lung and spleen channels and is strengthening to the yang *Qi*. As mentioned in the section on yin and yang (pages 86-7), the nature of yang tends to be hot, bright, upward and active. One of the uses of astragalus is for the treatment of prolapses, to help raise the descending energy which is pulling the organ downwards. Its sweet taste means that it is strengthening and nourishing. By entering the lung and spleen channels it is very helpful in enhancing the immune system and preventing illness.

It is more common to use several Chinese herbs in combination than it is to use them on their own. Chinese herbal formulae combine different herbs that work together effectively and in balance. One of the favourite ways of understanding prescriptions was based on the political structure of the Chinese dynasty. The name of the Chinese formulae known as the four gentlemen decoction (*Si Jun Zi Tang*) was derived from the Confucian term for a person whose behaviour is exemplary and the number four which is considered harmonious. It is a simple, moderate prescription of four herbs used to strengthen digestion and tonify *Qi*. The chief herb, also known as the "emperor" or *Jun* herb, is ginseng (*Ren Shen*), which is a powerful tonic for the digestion and overall energy. The "minister" or *Chen* herb – white *Atractylodes* rhizome (*Bai Zhu*) – acts as the adviser. These two herbs work synergistically to improve the digestive function. The "assistant" or *Zuo* herb is poria (*Fu Ling*) which is for strengthening and drying, and prevents the prescription from becoming too cloying and bloating. It combines well with the "envoy" or *Shi* herb, honey-fried licorice (*Zhi Gan Cao*) whose function it is to deliver the whole prescription to the digestive tract.

Chinese Patent Remedies are classical prescriptions made into pill form. This is a more convenient way to take the herbs, though generally they are not as strong as those prepared as decoctions. Different herbal companies produce variations on these prescriptions which will be called by other names, but the original formula should be stated. Many modern herbal companies are attempting to expand on the traditional formulae to focus their actions on long-term illnesses, especially AIDS and cancer. Hopefully with these new insights into the wisdom of the past, more successful treatments, or better still, ways of preventing these illnesses from taking hold in the first place will be found.

For centuries the Chinese have practised herbal medicine, providing many cures which have been adapted to treat modern illnesses.

Chinese herbal formulae are a combination of herbs which work together in a balanced and harmonious way.

SPECIFIC APPLICATIONS

Herbs form part of the spectrum of natural or energetic medicine, and as such, like all holistic methods, they are best used preventatively. For example, by treating a cold or flu in its early stages, you should be able to prevent a chest infection or bronchitis; similarly, tackling the symptoms of indigestion early may deter the development of a peptic ulcer. Most people feel happier and more whole when they are taking responsibility for their own health and have some control over what they put into their bodies, and quite often the judicious use of herbs can prevent a visit to the doctor altogether. However, when the symptoms are serious or intractable, seeking professional advice is then obviously a sensible course of action.

Where appropriate in this section, other areas of complementary medicine that have been found helpful for specific complaints are mentioned, and of course everyone should use their own judgement as to when to consult a doctor. There is no doubt that modern medicine saves lives, and drugs such as antibiotics have a valuable place in the case of severe infection; however, their indiscriminate use is harmful to the digestive tract and the immune system. If you have to resort to allopathic medicine, herbs may be very successful in alleviating any side effects or unpleasant consequences.

Evening primrose
(Oenothera biennis)

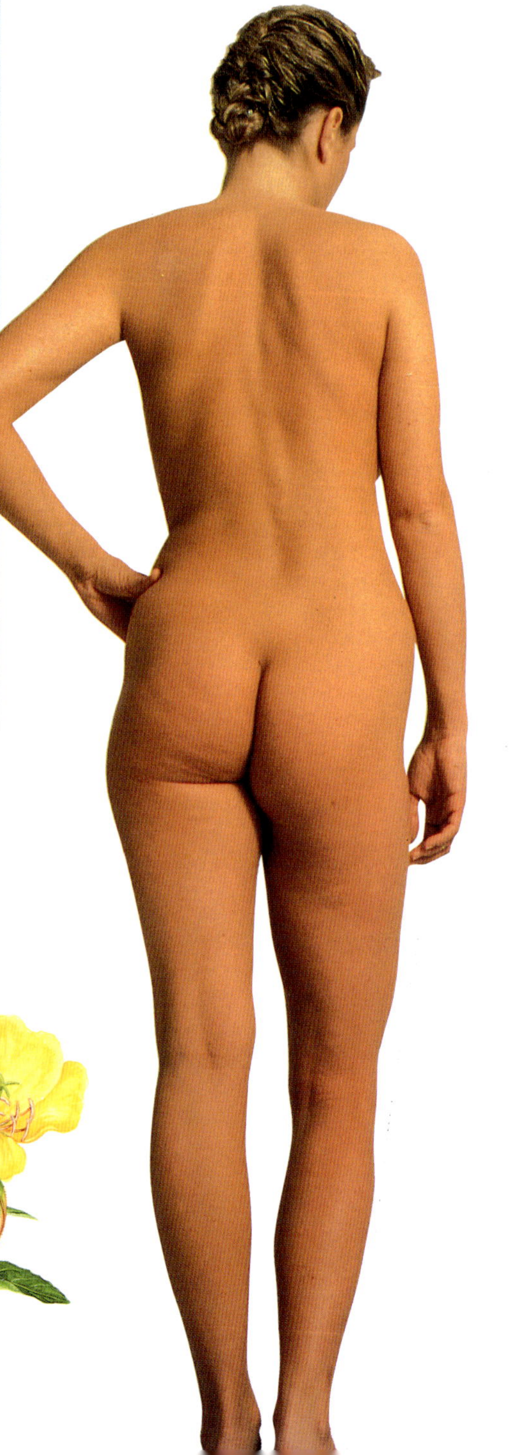

This section is arranged in order of the systems of the body:

Marigold
(Calendula officinalis)

THE HEAD AND CHEST

pages 92-97

This first section looks at common viral conditions affecting the respiratory tract, such as coughs and colds, sore throats and influenza. Herbs for more chronic problems such as migraine, heachache and rhinitis (hay fever) are also discussed.

THE DIGESTIVE SYSTEM

pages 98-101

Herbal medicine can be extremely useful for dealing with discomfort of the digestive tract. This section deals with a range of problems including heartburn, nausea, diarrhoea, constipation and irritable bowel syndrome.

Fennel
(Foeniculum vulgare)

Rose
(Rosa gallica officinalis)

THE REPRODUCTIVE AND URINARY SYSTEMS

pages 102-107

You can use herbs to facilitate smoother functioning of the reproductive organs, helping to make the important times of transition in women's lives – puberty, childbirth and menopause – more positive events.

WHOLE BODY AND SKIN

pages 108-113

This section deals with complaints which can affect all or part of the body: painful conditions, rashes and tiredness. This includes herbs for problems such as arthritis, rheumatism, post-viral fatigue, eczema and acne.

Licorice
(Glycyrrhiza glabra)

RECOMMENDED HERBS

After finding out the herbs recommended for a particular problem, you should then cross-check in the section on the herbs and their actions (pages 70-79), to ensure that they are suitable for you and your symptoms.

Finally, having selected the herbs you want to use, remember to mix and prepare them carefully and consciously, keeping in your awareness that they are part of the Planet's resources and as such, to be used with respect and care.

EMOTIONS

pages 114-117

Anyone can be affected by stress, anxiety or sleeplessness at various times in their lives. Herbs cannot eliminate the problems you face, but may enable you to deal with them more easily. A number of herbs are included which are calming, facilitate sleep or alleviate depression. However, we recommend you consult your doctor, counsellor or therapist if your emotional problems persist.

Passion-flower
(Passiflora incarnata)

Head and Chest

Illnesses that affect the head and the chest are the very common conditions that usually people get at least once a year. The Chinese would say that the head and neck, being at the top of the body and often the most exposed to cold winds and wet weather, are where disease first enters the body. In the West it is accepted that viruses travel through the air so it is often in the respiratory system that they take hold.

A few simple herbs can give much relief without the need for other medication, especially if they are taken early on. Many people find that herbs are the most effective way of treating catarrhal conditions – far better than antibiotics. Of course, if you have a high fever, pain, or a condition which is not clearing, you must seek professional medical advice. If you do need to take antibiotics, it is fine to continue to take the herbs listed.

Common Cold

Colds are often seen as a nuisance. Actually, they are your body's way of saying it is tired and needs a break. A cold is a good time for the body to thoroughly clear out all the toxins that have accumulated through daily life. These processes can be helped by resting, drinking lots of liquids and eating lightly, and taking vitamin C and herbs.

Peppermint
(Mentha piperata)

Yarrow
(Achillea millefolium)

Elderflower, Peppermint and Yarrow

These herbs are aromatic and drying; very useful for the early stage of a cold. Drink decoctions as hot as possible, every few hours. They will help to clear your head and dry up your runny nose.

Boneset and Nepeta

These herbs help to clear mild fevers and to ease the aches and pains of flu. Combine with other herbs as needed. Generally, a fever with sweating is a good way of getting rid of a cold and these herbs will promote perspiration. This will then cause the fever to "break" and the temperature will start to go down.

Honeysuckle
(Lonicera)

Yin Qiao Jie Du Pien
This Chinese patent remedy has an excellent reputation for getting rid of colds. It has to be taken at the first signs of a cold, before it is established. Take 5 pills every 2–3 hours with a warm drink.

Honeysuckle and forsythia are the main ingredients of this formula. They are used to clear mild chills and fever, headache, thirst and cough. Take as an infusion with 1 tsp of each herb in a pot of boiled water. Sweeten with honey.

SORE THROAT

Often a sore throat is the first indication of a cold. Plenty of rest and drinking lots of liquids should help it to pass quickly. If it continues, and is very painful with swollen glands, there is the chance that it has turned into a throat infection and may need professional treatment.

Marigold
(Calendula officinalis)

ECHINACEA, CLEAVERS AND MARIGOLD

These herbs will help with more persistent and infected sore throats. Echinacea is excellent for fighting infections and is often taken as a tincture. It is advisable for adults to take at least 1 tsp two or three times a day with a severe infection, and it is safe to use in smaller doses for children.

Cleavers and marigold will also help to clear infections from the lymphatic system and can be taken in combination as a tea or tincture.

Red Sage
(Salvia officinalis)

RED SAGE

Use this as a gargle by making an infusion of 1 heaped tsp of sage for 1 cup of water. It can also be drunk as a soothing tea.

COUGHS

There are many different types of coughs and each type needs its own remedy. Often one type of cough will turn into another one, and this can be very confusing. It is worthwhile trying to find the right remedy because herbs are very good at clearing coughs, especially those that are very persistent. Chronic coughs can indicate a lung weakness which acupuncture may be able to strengthen.

COLTSFOOT, HYSSOP AND ELECAMPANE

These herbs will help clear a loose, phlegmy cough. Add some echinacea tincture if the catarrh is green; this indicates there is an infection.

Comfrey
(Symphytum officinale)

GINGER, HONEY AND LEMON

This traditional remedy is simple but effective in treating coughs with lots of clear mucus.

> ### GOLDEN SEAL
> Is another great herb for moving and drying phlegm. It should be used in smaller doses and *avoided during pregnancy*.

MARSHMALLOW, COLTSFOOT, MULLEIN AND COMFREY

These herbs will soothe dry, irritating coughs. Add honey or licorice to sweeten and moisten.

THYME AND WILD CHERRY

These herbs are very soothing and useful with spasms of coughing, especially those that keep you awake at night. Thyme can be added to the bath or use a few drops of thyme oil on your pillow to help relax the lungs.

Earaches

For the initial stages of earache where pain is mild and fever is low or non-existent, the following herbs are very useful. If pain is extreme with a high fever and purulent discharge coming from the ear, it is best to seek medical help immediately. Avoid putting any drops into the ear if the eardrum has burst.

Echinacea
(Echinacea angustifolia)

Chamomile
(Anthemis nobilis)

Chamomile, Skullcap, Hyssop and Echinacea

Drink as a medicinal tea three times a day to help clear the infection and soothe the pain.

Garlic, Lavender and Olive Oil

This mixture makes excellent eardrops. Slice the garlic and place in a small amount of olive oil with a few lavender flowers. Leave for 2 hours. Strain. Warm 1 tsp of the oil by placing it over a cup of hot water. Put a few drops into the sore ear and plug with some cotton wool.

Eye Complaints

Here are a few suggestions for herbal teas that will help with dry, red and irritated eyes. If you make an eye wash, it is important to make it as a decoction and to use sterilized containers to prevent infection from spreading.

Eyebright

This is an excellent herb used to strengthen and heal almost all eye ailments. It can be made into an eye wash or taken internally as a tea. Add chamomile or marigold to help soothe sore eyes. Or use cold chamomile tea bags on the eyes as a simple compress to clear red, irritated eyes.

Eyebright
(Euphrasia officinalis)

Chrysanthemum

(*Ju Hua*, Chinese Chrysanthemum)
This is useful for sore, red, irritated eyes. Drink as a tea, use as an eye wash or make a compress with the teabags. It is also helpful for eye problems related to headaches. There is a patent formula called *Qi Ju Di Huang Wan* which contains *Ju Hua*. This helps to strengthen and brighten eyes especially if there are feelings of general tiredness. Older people with chronic eye conditions may also find it helpful.

HEADACHES AND MIGRAINE

There are many different types of headaches, with migraines possibly being the most extreme. The cause of the headache is important to sort out. This could be eye strain, back problems, allergies, sinusitis or hormonal imbalances, to name a few. Tension and overwork can also cause headaches, and if this is the case, try to take some time off for rest and relaxation.

Herbal baths using a strong infusion of oils can make the whole process of unwinding deliciously pleasant! Massaging relaxing oils such as lavender, peppermint or marjoram into the head, neck and feet can ease muscle tensions and bring great relief.

Chamomile, feverfew, lavender, lemon balm, marjoram, meadowsweet, peppermint, rosemary, skullcap, thyme, valerian and vervain are just a few herbs useful for headache pain, depending on the underlying cause. Try them on their own or mix several together. Look them up in the herbal section (pages 70-9) to find out what suits you best.

Herbal baths using a strong infusion of oils can make the whole process of unwinding deliciously pleasant!

Passion-flower
(Passiflora incarnata)

SKULLCAP, VALERIAN AND PASSION-FLOWER

Use these very effective herbs for pain relief and to ease stress and tension.

AGNUS CASTUS AND WILD YAM

If headaches are related to the menstrual cycle, these herbs can be added to any listed here. They will need to be taken over several months to re-establish hormonal balance.

Feverfew
(Tanacetum parthenium)

LEMON BALM, LAVENDER AND MEADOWSWEET

This is a good herbal mixture if the headaches are related to digestive upsets.

Lavender
(Lavandula officinalis)

LEMON BALM, FEVERFEW, MEADOWSWEET AND ROSEMARY

Combine these herbs in infusions and drink 3 cups daily if you are prone to migraines. Migraines can also be brought on by allergies to certain foods, low blood sugar, stress, hormonal imbalances and postural problems, so it is important to check these out!

HAY FEVER

Allergies to grasses and pollens can cause great discomfort. To prevent the hay fever occurring and to be really effective, start treatment a month before your particular hay fever season begins. This will help to tone up your system before the allergens hit the air, and your nose! It may be necessary to go on a low-mucus diet, avoiding foods which increase catarrh such as cheese, eggs, milk, bananas and peanut butter. Vitamin C, zinc and garlic will build up your resistance, so it may help to take these supplements. Acupuncture treatment is also helpful in strengthening and clearing your system so allergic reactions are less severe.

Garlic
(Allium sativum)

Echinacea
(Echinacea angustifolia)

ECHINACEA, ELDERFLOWER, EYEBRIGHT AND HYSSOP

Combine in equal quantities and make a tea to drink three times a day.

Herbal remedies can help to alleviate many of the uncomfortable symptoms which plague allergy sufferers.

CHAMOMILE AND EYEBRIGHT

Make a decoction and use it to bathe the eyes.

Elderflower
(Sambucus nigra)

Bi Yan Pian
This Chinese patent remedy is excellent for clearing the congestion of hay fever. Take it with the first symptoms of hay fever and it will help to stop them from developing. It is best to take the pills after meals.

SINUSITIS

Inflammation of the sinus cavities can lead to an over-production of mucus. This can create pain above or behind the eyes, and stuffiness. Chronic sinusitis can be aggravated by colds, hay fever and damp weather. A low-mucus diet and supplements (see suggestions for hay fever opposite) is recommended. Acupuncture treatment is also very successful with treating sinusitis. A high fever and severe pain may indicate that there is an infection and medical help is advised.

ECHINACEA, EYEBRIGHT, ELDERFLOWER, GOLDEN SEAL AND MARSHMALLOW

These herbs taken as a tea or tincture are very effective at clearing catarrh and soothing irritated membranes in the nose.

Elderflower is very effective at drying up mucus and fighting infections.

PALPITATIONS

Irregular or forcible heartbeats can have many different causes such as allergies, menopause, fear, sexual excitement, and over-consumption of coffee and smoking cigarettes. Although they can't help the underlying cause (only some behaviour changes can do that), herbal remedies can help to reduce erratic and fast heartbeats and stop them from damaging the heart.

LEMON BALM, LIME BLOSSOM, MOTHERWORT AND PASSION-FLOWER

Take this infusion to help with palpitations with signs of stress and anxiety.

Lime blossom
(Tilia europea)

Motherwort
(Leonurus cardiaca)

HAWTHORN BERRIES

These berries are very helpful in regulating the heartbeat, normalizing heart function, and strengthening the cardiovascular system. Add them if there are any signs of high blood pressure or heart problems.

DIGESTIVE SYSTEM

Eating should be one of life's many pleasures. Problems with digestion can create discomfort which then begins to affect all aspects of daily life. It is best to listen to the body and sort out digestive complaints while symptoms are still mild. This can help to prevent more serious digestive ailments which are often painful, difficult to cure, and very debilitating. Herbs for the more chronic condition of irritable bowel syndrome are suggested, although this may need professional treatment.

A healthy diet and regular meals are important means of helping any problem that relates to digestion, and this is an essential part of treatment. Good digestion thrives on relaxed, peaceful mealtimes. As well as eating healthily and regularly, take some time to enjoy your food.

INDIGESTION AND HEARTBURN

Stomach discomfort, gas and acidity can be the result of too many rich, fatty, or spicy foods; drinking too much tea, coffee or alcohol; or smoking cigarettes. Stress, tension, and rushed mealtimes can also affect the digestion. If you already eat in a healthy, regular and relaxed manner and still feel unwell, try the following herbal remedies.

Meadowsweet
(Filipendula ulmaria)

Fennel
(Foeniculum vulgare)

CARDAMOM, PEPPERMINT AND FENNEL

Take these herbs after eating to aid digestion and settle the stomach. They also help to clear wind and bloating. The more traditional after-dinner mint or Indian cardamom tea may be based on this knowledge.

SLIPPERY ELM

This can be taken in tablet form or powder and has the effect of soothing the stomach lining. Take the powder mixed in hot water and sweetened with honey or blackcurrant cordial. It has an unusual taste and texture, but does work very well to ease acid indigestion and stop pain. It is also very nourishing to the digestive system.

MEADOWSWEET, COMFREY AND MARSHMALLOW

These herbs also help to heal a sensitive stomach lining. Take as a combination or individually.

CHAMOMILE, ROSEMARY AND LEMON BALM

These relaxing herbs aid digestion and are especially useful if there is susceptibility to nervous upsets.

NAUSEA

Nausea can be the result of many different conditions, and once again, it is important to establish the underlying cause.

GINGER, CHAMOMILE, FENNEL AND PEPPERMINT

To help settle the stomach, try sipping these herbal teas slowly. They are all mild, safe herbs so they can be used with children for travel sickness and illness. They are also fine to use for morning sickness for pregnant women. Try peppermint sweets or ginger biscuits for a treat.

TANGERINE PEEL *(Chen Pi)*

This fragrant Chinese herb has many uses for digestive disorders and eases nausea as well as feelings of fullness and bloating. It helps to strengthen the digestion and send the food downwards. Take as a tea or a tincture in warm water after meals. It is interesting that citrus peel is used in the West in rich fruit cakes, maybe to help us digest them better!

LEMON BALM, HOPS AND PASSION-FLOWER

These herbs will help to calm the stomach and are useful if nervous tension is present. Usually they are taken with some of the herbs listed here as either a tea or a tincture.

ABDOMINAL PAIN AND BLOATING

Abdominal pain and bloating can be indications of a variety of digestive disturbances. It is important to understand the underlying cause which can be anything from a weak, nervous digestion, food allergies, or bad eating habits, to more complicated conditions such as ulcers, gallstones, or irritable bowel syndrome.

If a person has food sensitivities, certain herbs may be aggravating. Use them in small amounts at first. Daily massage of the lower abdomen in a clockwise direction starting from the centre and moving outwards may help. There is also a wide variety of nutritional supplements that aid digestion.

WILD YAM, PEPPERMINT, GINGER, CINNAMON, FENNEL, LEMON BALM AND CHAMOMILE

These herbs are good for clearing wind and easing bloating. Drink a cup of one of these herbal teas after meals, or take a few drops of the tincture in some warm water.

Caraway seeds

Cayenne

Cardamom

CAYENNE, GINGER, CARDAMOM AND CARAWAY SEEDS

Add these warming spices to your cooking but avoid using them if you are suffering from ulcers or irritable bowel syndrome.

Ginger *(Zingiber offinale)*

Xiang Sha Liu Jun Wan

This Chinese patent formula contains herbs to strengthen the digestion and alleviate pain and distension. It is also indicated for reduced appetite, feelings of fullness after eating small amounts, belching, and sometimes nausea and diarrhoea. Avoid using long term if there is thirst, irritability and constipation as it may be too warming.

CONSTIPATION

Constipation is not a disease but a symptom of other problems. A good diet should include foods that contain fibre. This is found in many fruits and vegetables as well as in wholemeal bread, cereals, nuts and seeds. Avoid refined foods such as white bread, cakes and sweets. Dairy products, especially hard cheeses, can also be clogging. Stress and tension affect the digestion and there may be a tendency to "hold on" to things psychologically and physically. Relaxation classes or a break from our usual routines may be a positive solution.

Medication may have constipation as a side effect, and it is always important to be aware of this when taking any drugs. Long-term use of laxatives is potentially harmful to the digestion as they do not encourage the peristaltic movement of the intestines and may "push" the food through without its goodness being absorbed fully. As with most digestive problems, it is important to eat regularly and drink plenty of liquids. Physical exercise, even walking, will help to keep the system moving.

WATER AND LEMON JUICE

This simple combination taken first thing in the morning, half an hour before any food is eaten can really help and is worth trying!

PSYLLIUM SEEDS AND LINSEED

Put 1–2 tsp of seeds in a cup of hot water. Let them soak for 2 hours. Sweeten with lemon and honey and drink. Alternatively, sprinkle the seeds on cereal for breakfast. Linseeds are also rich in oils that are used to help moisturize hair and skin, so they have the added benefit of enhancing our beauty!

Licorice
(Glycyrrhiza glabra)

RHUBARB ROOT

Taken in small doses, it helps to tone the intestines and promote appetite. In large doses it purges – this should be avoided except in extreme cases. Please note that this is not the same as garden rhubarb, and it may colour the urine yellow or red. *Use with caution in pregnancy, definitely avoiding large doses.*

Dandelion root
(Taraxacum officinale)

LICORICE, GINGER, DANDELION ROOT, YELLOW DOCK ROOT AND BURDOCK

If constipation does not respond to changes in diet and the suggestions above, try a mixture of these herbs. Substitute fennel for ginger if there is a lot of wind and colic.

DIARRHOEA

This condition may be due to an acute gastric infection, or it may be more long term in cases where there is a weakness in the digestive system. Stress, anxiety and new situations may also affect the bowels, causing diarrhoea. Generally, it is best to eat plain foods and avoid alcohol, coffee, dairy products, and spicy or rich foods. Better still, in acute cases try to avoid eating for 24 hours, but drink plenty of liquids and teas. If the diarrhoea is severe or persistent, it is necessary to get medical help, especially with children. With bouts of diarrhoea, it maybe necessary to re-mineralize the body and taking "Dioralyte" will help replace lost mineral salts and prevent dehydration. Water, mixed with small amounts of baking soda and sugar, will also work.

MEADOWSWEET

Take frequently as a tea or tincture. It will help to settle the stomach and stop diarrhoea. It is safe to use with children.

CHAMOMILE AND LEMON BALM

These herbs are used to help relaxation and can be added to meadowsweet to ease diarrhoea due to anxiety and nervousness.

Si Jun Zi Tang
("Four gentlemen decoction")
This Chinese prescription can be taken as a decoction, tincture or powder. It is mild in nature and is strengthening to the digestion and general energy. It is best taken over a long period of time.

BAYBERRY, AGRIMONY AND COMFREY ROOT

This mixture is useful to stop diarrhoea for adults. Add ginger root and camomile to soothe griping pains. Add marshmallow to help ease symptoms of acidity and inflammation.

SAGE

Drink sage tea after a light meal to aid digestion and reduce diarrhoea.

IRRITABLE BOWEL SYNDROME

This common complaint has varying symptoms for each individual who suffers from it. Often there is alternating diarrhoea and constipation with flatulence and discomfort. It may be a result of stress and bad eating habits. It could also be caused by allergic reactions to certain foods. These food intolerances are different with each person but common ones are tea, coffee, wheat, and dairy products. It is often difficult to discover food allergies, and even more difficult to avoid them, especially if they are ones found in commonly eaten foods such as wheat.

The best procedure is to cut out one food at a time for 10 days. Gradually reintroduce it back into the diet noting any reactions. It may be best to consult a nutritionist especially if allergies are severe.

SLIPPERY ELM

This is a favourite for most digestive problems because it is soothing and nourishing. Take three times a day as a gruel using 1 tsp per cup of hot water. Sweeten with honey or blackcurrant.

WILD YAM, CHAMOMILE, PEPPERMINT, AGRIMONY, MARSHMALLOW AND GOLDEN SEAL

Drink a cup of these herbs three to six times a day to soothe the bowel and stop inflammation. Add the golden seal as a tincture as the smell of the powder can be off putting to drink. *Do not use golden seal if you are pregnant as it stimulates the uterus.*

LIME BLOSSOM, SKULLCAP AND HOPS

Add one or more of these herbs to the above mixture for Irritable Bowel Syndrome if stress is increasing bowel problems. Avoid using hops if suffering from depression.

Reproductive and Urinary Systems

Most women's lives will be affected by changes in their reproductive systems. The onset of menstruation, pregnancy and birth, and the time of the menopause are strong influences over their feelings of sexuality and growth. They may be the markers of important cycles of change.

In this section herbs are included that will help women to adjust to these changes more easily. In addition, there are some useful herbs for cystitis which is not necessarily linked to the reproductive system but is common in women.

Premenstrual Tension

Premenstrual tension (PMT) is widely recognized today, and it is generally accepted that hormones can affect emotional states. The symptoms and duration of (PMT) will vary from woman to woman. Symptoms can include emotional instability, lack of co-ordination, water retention, painful breasts, headaches, nausea, and skin changes (see relevant sections on pages 95 and 108).

Diet supplements, like evening primrose oil, magnesium, calcium, and vitamin B may be useful. Acupuncture treatment taken over several months is very effective and a great way to unwind.

Xiao Yao San
This Chinese patent formula helps to ease general symptoms of (PMT) especially if there are digestive problems the week before the period. If there are symptoms of weakness and tiredness, take "Women's precious pills" (see page 79) when the bleeding has stopped. Continue these until the week before the period, when *Xiao Yao San* is taken again. Take the combination of patent formulae for three months to help regulate the menstrual cycle.

Agnus castus

This herb helps to stabilize the hormones. Combine and make a decoction to drink three times a day as a course of treatment for three months. Tinctures and pills are also available and easier to use. It is important to take this herb daily.

Dandelion *(Taraxacum officinale)*

Motherwort, skullcap and passion-flower

These herbs help to ease feelings of stress and anxiety. Decoct valerian root, or add as a tincture, if there is muscle tension through the neck and shoulders, but avoid long-term use of this herb.

Parsley *(Petroselinum crispum)*

Dandelion leaves and parsley

These herbs will act as a diuretic to ease water retention. Combine and infuse to make a tea to be drunk when needed.

Dysmenorrhoea

Painful periods are a very common complaint. Most often the pain is disruptive and uncomfortable, and herbs can be a natural way of easing it. Pain at the beginning of the bleeding is often due to the reduction of blood flow by spasms of the uterus. Pain lasting throughout the period is more often due to congestion within the uterus. If pain is severely uncomfortable, if there is heavy bleeding or if there are signs of infection mid-cycle (ie if there is pain, fever or smelly discharge), it is important to seek medical advice immediately and consult a qualified herbal practitioner.

Agnus castus, false unicorn root, motherwort and squaw vine

These herbs help to balance the hormones and to tonify the uterus. Combine and drink three times a day for six weeks.

Marigold
(Calendula officinalis)

Wild yam, crampbark, pasque flower, marigold and raspberry leaf

For period pain, combine and drink three times a day when needed.

Raspberry leaf, marigold, nettles and shepherd's purse

For heavy bleeding or bleeding between periods, pour a cup of boiling water on to 1–2 tsp of dried herbs. Infuse for 10 minutes and drink every 2–3 hours just before and during a period.

Ginger, cinnamon and cloves

Pain can also be due to cold and these pungent herbs can warm the uterus and help the blood to flow more easily. Add these to a tea, or better still, make a mulled wine.

Amenorrhoea

Amenorrhoea is the condition in which menstruation does not occur. This can be due to physical exhaustion, stress and anxiety, weight loss for any reason, hormonal dysfunction or when stopping use of the contraceptive pill (because the body may take some time to regain its natural rhythms). However, it may also be due to an underlying physical condition. Because of this, and because these herbs might harm an unknown pregnancy, *it is extremely important that you check with your doctor before using any of these remedies, to assure that the reproductive system is in a normal, non-pregnant state.*

Pennyroyal and tansy

For treating regular menstrual cycle with occasionally delayed menstruation, infuse and drink three times a day until the period begins.

Agnus castus, false unicorn root, blue cohosh, rue and motherwort

These herbs will help to regulate hormonal activity, strengthen the uterus and bring on delayed or suppressed menstruation. Decoct and drink three times a day.

Dang gui bu xue tang

This Chinese patent remedy helps to nourish the blood. Take over several months if there is anaemia, paleness and tiredness with little or no menstrual bleeding.

Pennyroyal
(Mentha pulegium)

Licorice, black cohosh, agnus castus and motherwort

If stopping use of the contraceptive pill, these herbs will benefit the adrenal glands, tone the uterus and normalize hormonal function. After coming off the pill, decoct and drink three times a day for the first week, twice a day for the second week, and once a day for the third week.

Rue
(Ruta graveolens)

SUB-FERTILITY

Problems in conceiving are on the increase and it is well worth trying acupuncture, homeopathy, and herbal and nutritional therapies. A qualified practitioner should be consulted if you do not have good results with these herbs after several months.

Rose
(Rosa gallica)

DAMIANA, SAW PALMETTO, CELERY SEEDS, OATS, LICORICE AND GINGER

These herbs will help to raise a low sperm count and help to strengthen the male reproductive system. It is also important to eat well, and avoid alcohol, cigarettes, caffeine, tight clothes and hot baths.

FALSE UNICORN ROOT, ROSES, NETTLE AND MARIGOLD

These herbs will help to balance hormones and nourish the blood and uterus. Take over several months and follow the advice suggested above. Vitamin B, royal jelly, Floradix, kelp, and evening primrose oil may also be helpful depending on your state of health.

Marigold
(Calendula officinalis)

Nettle
(Urtica dioica)

Vervain
(Verbena officinalis)

NETTLE, SKULLCAP, VERVAIN, DANDELION ROOT AND PRICKLY ASH

For low vitality and stress, add a combination of these herbs to enhance the effects of those listed above.

Pregnancy, Birth and Postnatal Care

Herbal treatment for pregnancy, birth, and postnatal care has a very rich and valuable tradition. For centuries, midwives have used herbs to help women maintain a healthy pregnancy, ease birth and support postnatal care. Many of the herbs used in this section for the healing of women and aiding the birthing process have come from the different tribes of the Native Americans. Herbs such as squaw vine, black cohosh, blue cohosh and false unicorn root are invaluable complements to European remedies. While it is best to avoid medication with pregnancy, some herbs may be very beneficial.

HERBS TO BE AVOIDED DURING PREGNANCY:
Some herbs have a stimulating action on the uterus which may result in miscarriage, the most common of which are aloes, autumn crocus, barberry, golden seal, juniper, male fern, mandrake, pennyroyal, poke root, rhubarb, rue, sage, southernwood, tansy, thuja and wormwood.

CHAMOMILE, LEMON BALM AND MEADOWSWEET

A mixture of these herbs, or the use of any one of them, may help to settle the stomach if suffering from morning sickness. Take as an infusion when needed.

PEPPERMINT, FENNEL, GINGER AND CINNAMON

These herbs are warming to the digestion and may also help to settle the stomach if suffering from morning sickness. Take the peppermint or fennel on their own, or add any one of these herbs to another tea. For example, try adding a couple of slices of ginger root to a pot of meadowsweet tea.

RASPBERRY LEAF AND SQUAW VINE

These herbs help to strengthen the uterus and prepare for birth. Take 1 tsp of one herb or combine ½ tsp of both herbs per cup and drink an infusion once or twice a day during the last three months of pregnancy.

BLACK COHOSH, BLUE COHOSH AND GOLDEN SEAL

These herbs help to strengthen weak contractions during labour. Take a mixture with some ginger.

BLUE COHOSH, WILD YAM, CRAMPBARK, RASPBERRY LEAVES AND SQUAW VINE

For short, sharp contractions during labour with tension and pain and a rigid cervix, take these herbs as a tea or tincture.

Nu Ke Ba Zhen Wan
("Women's precious pills")
Take 5 tablets three times a day to help revitalize and nourish after the birth.

COMFREY, MARIGOLD AND ST JOHN'S WORT

Use 1 tbsp of herbs to 600ml (1 pt) of water for a soothing and healing bath after the birth.

Fennel
(Foeniculum vulgare)

NETTLES, FENNEL, VERVAIN, BORAGE, RASPBERRY LEAVES OR MARSHMALLOW

Take any of these herbs individually or in combination to help increase milk production. Drink one cup three times a day.

CHINESE ANGELICA AND ASTRAGALUS

These two herbs in combination help to nourish the blood and strengthen the *Qi* (vital force). This is especially important if the labour has been long and difficult or there has been much loss of blood. Traditionally, the *Dang Gui* was cooked with a chicken and the meat and juices were used to nourish the new mother. The herbs also come prepared as a patent formula called *Dang Gui Bu Xue Tang*.

COMFREY, CHICKWEED OR MARIGOLD-CALENDULA OINTMENTS

Rub into sore, cracked nipples for relief.

Menopausal Discomforts

The menopause is an important time of change and transition. Its onset may be gradual with periods coming less frequently, or it may occur quite suddenly. In most cases there are also many emotional adjustments to make. Issues such as ageing, children leaving home, and career decisions may need to be faced. Physically, there are changes in the pituitary and ovarian hormone levels due to the ovaries no longer releasing the ovum. Discomforts commonly experienced are hot flushes, palpitations, irritability, depression, insomnia, joint pain and general debility. Any severe discomforts or excessive bleeding require medical attention. Constitutional treatment and emotional support from a qualified practitioner or therapist may be useful.

By easing the physical discomforts that may occur during the menopause, an older woman can cope with other changes in her life.

Sage and Blackcurrant Leaves

These herbs taken as a tea will help to reduce symptoms of hot flushes.

Sage
(Salvia officinalis)

Skullcap, Vervain and Lime Blossom

Use this gentle herbal combination to ease nervousness, anxiety, depression and mood swings. They may be added to other herbal combinations depending on your symptoms.

Agnus Castus, False Unicorn Root, Wild Yam, St John's Wort, Chinese Angelica and Motherwort

Herbal combination used to establish a new level of hormonal function.

Decoct and drink three times a day for three months.

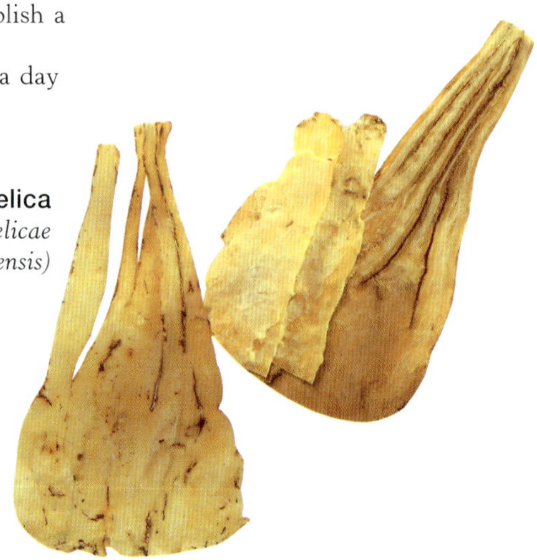

Chinese angelica
(Radix angelicae sinensis)

Cystitis

This urinary tract infection can be caused by inflammation in the bladder and/or urethra. Symptoms may be an urgency and frequency of urination, with pain or a burning sensation. Drink plenty of water, adding 1 tsp of baking soda twice a day. *Do not do this if you have a heart problem.*
Avoid coffee, tea, alcohol, spicy foods, citrus fruits and cigarettes. If there is fever, low back pain, bloody or cloudy urine, it is important to get medical attention as there is a chance of a kidney infection. If you have recurrent bouts of cystitis, professional help may be needed.

Buchu, cornsilk, couchgrass and marshmallow leaves

Combine, infuse and drink a cupful every two hours.

Marshmallow
(Althaea officinalis)

Irritating drinks such as coffee will increase the pain and inflammation in the bladder.

Barley water

Simmer 113g (4oz) of washed pot barley in 600ml (1 pt) of water until the barley is soft. Strain and add honey and lemon. Drink as needed.

Chamomile
(Anthemis nobilis)

Whole Body and Skin

This section covers ailments which may affect the whole body. To treat these conditions effectively, the body has to be led back to a state of health and balance. One of the major causes of rheumatism and arthritis is the accumulation of toxins or waste products in the joints. Although only one or two joints may be painful, it may be necessary to look at what is going on in the whole body in order to find a cure.

Fatigue, tiredness and aching muscles can also be due to the body gradually becoming more toxic and sensitive to foods, pollution and stress. Myalgic encephalomyelitis (ME), post-viral syndrome, and chronic Epstein Barr virus disease are all conditions in which fatigue is the major disability. Their causes are not clear, but complementary medicine can offer relief and hope.

Arthritis and Rheumatism

These painful conditions have many forms varying from hot, swollen, painful joints to stiff and difficult movements. It may be necessary to have a good osteopathic treatment to check the alignment of the bones and muscles.

Food allergies can eventually cause a build-up of toxicity in the joints. Acidic reactions are caused by red meat, eggs, dairy products, vinegars, pickles, refined sugars and most spices. Foods rich in oxalic acid, such as rhubarb, gooseberries, and black and red currants, should also be avoided. Coffee, black tea, alcohol, sugar and salt can also contribute to the accumulation of toxins, and are detrimental to a cleansing process. Instead eat plenty of whole grains and vegetables (exclude tomatoes, although this is technically a fruit). Drink at least 1.8l (3 pt) of water/liquid a day to flush the system. Take cod liver oil, evening primrose oil, kelp and selenium to help repair bones and cartilage.

Yellow Dock and Licorice

Constipation can increase the build-up of toxicity, making regular bowel movements important. If this is a problem, add these herbs to the celery seed, burdock, meadowsweet and yarrow tea.

Finally, it is worth mentioning that our body is affected by our mental state. Stress and tension can restrict our movements and circulation, stopping muscles and joints from getting the exercise and blood flow that they need. Yoga, Tai Chi, and any other gentle activity will help increase mobility and alleviate stiffness. Acupuncture can also be very effective in removing pain and stiffness. As with any other ailment, if you are in a great deal of pain and discomfort, please seek professional medical care.

Celery Seed, Burdock, Meadowsweet and Yarrow

These herbs help to cleanse the system. Take this tea over a long period of time.

Black Cohosh and Blue Cohosh

Add to the tea if symptoms are post-menopausal to help balance the hormones.

Yellow dock root and Licorice

JAMAICAN DOGWOOD, PASSION-FLOWER AND VALERIAN

These herbs will help if pain is preventing sleep. Take this tea or tincture half an hour before bedtime. It is a safe mixture and may be used in a slightly stronger dose than normal. *Avoid long-term use of valerian.*

Valerian *(Valeriana officinalis)*

NETTLES, HAWTHORN AND PRICKLY ASH

These herbs help improve circulation. Add to other herbs or use on their own if pain and stiffness have gone.

Hawthorn *(Crataegus oxyacanthoides)*

Passion-flower *(Passiflora incarnata)*

Peppermint *(Mentha piperata)*

ST JOHN'S WORT, PEPPERMINT AND LAVENDER OILS

Massage painful joints with these oils to help increase circulation and ease pain.

Lavender *(Lavandula officinalis)*

GREEN CABBAGE LEAVES AND COMFREY LEAVES

Wrap hot, swollen, painful joints in these to help relieve swelling and pain.

Chronic Tiredness and Fatigue

Chronic tiredness can be the result of many different conditions. In order to treat it effectively, it is important to find out the cause, or at least eliminate some of the possibilities! A physical examination by a doctor, including blood tests, is necessary especially if the fatigue is severe. Take a good look at the possibility of overworking and emotional stress being the causes. Maybe it is important to take a long overdue holiday. Depression and fatigue are sometimes linked and it is hard to tell which came first. Try to sort out any long term stressful situations (see section on Emotions, pages 114-7). If tiredness is coming in waves during the day, it may be due to low blood sugar or food allergies.

Eating healthy, regular meals and avoiding excesses of caffeine, alcohol and sugar may be difficult to do at first, but well worth it in the long run. Sleeping difficulties need to be sorted out so that you wake rested and refreshed (see Insomnia. page 116). Regular exercise can help you to keep fit and strong. For many people, especially those with sedentary jobs, exercise has been found very revitalizing. However, if exercise makes you feel even more exhausted, stop doing it. ME, post-viral syndrome, and chronic Epstein-Barr virus have symptoms which will vary with each individual, but are generally made worse from exercise and lack of rest. Their acute phase may be like flu, which then develops into a more debilitating condition, the symptoms including fatigue, muscular aches, poor memory and concentration, sore throats, dizziness and digestive complaints.

Finally, if you are on any medication, check for any side effects of tiredness. The dosage or the drug may need to be altered but always check with the doctor first.

Cleavers
(Galium aparine)

Echinacea
(Echinacea angustifolia)

Echinacea, Yellow Dock Root, Cleavers, Marigold and Licorice

These herbs will help to cleanse the body and enhance the immune system. They are appropriate to take when tiredness is due to poor diet, over-indulgences in alcohol and caffeine, smoking, recurring infections, ME, or candidiasis. They can be taken as tea or tincture three times a day over several months if necessary.

Putting soothing herbs in the bath can aid restful sleep.

Marigold
(Calendula officinalis)

Ginseng
(Radix ginseng)

Regular exercise can be revitalising by helping to release stress and tension and increase the blood flow to all parts of the body.

GINSENG

This Chinese herb is renowned for its strengthening properties. It is very useful with any debility and can be taken for three-month periods. *Avoid if pregnant or with high blood pressure.* Use only if there is debility; it is inappropriate to use if you are well.

Si Jun Zi Tang
("Four gentlemen decoction")
This Chinese herbal formula is helpful to rebuild strength after a debilitating illness. Take as a decoction over a long period of time.

OATS, VERVAIN AND DANDELION

These herbs support the nervous system and help to cleanse the liver. They would be useful as a support after periods of stress and overwork.

Dandelion
(Taraxacum officinale)

Vervain
(Verbena officinalis)

Yu Ping Feng San
("Jade windscreen powder")
This Chinese herbal formula contains the herb astragalus (*Huang Qi*) which is being used to build up the immune system in chronic conditions like AIDS. The formula can be taken as a decoction, powder or tincture and is very useful as a protection against colds and flu.

Astragalus
(Radix astragali membranaceus)

Skin Conditions

The skin is a major organ which has the responsibility of protecting you from environmental factors and helps to eliminate internal waste products. Its condition can be affected by sun, age, foods, soaps and many other things. Here are a few suggestions for the treatment of common skin conditions. Some conditions, such as eczema and psoriasis, may need consultation with a trained herbal practitioner.

Eczema

There are many causes of eczema and these need to be investigated carefully. Allergic reactions to soaps, materials, animals and foods can aggravate it. Stress can also cause it to flare up. Underlying the condition may be some nutritional deficiencies.
It may be helpful to take evening primrose oil and a multi-vitamin and mineral supplement.

Red Clover, Borage, Burdock Root and Nettles

This is a basic remedy which can help heal the skin by cleansing and nourishing the blood. It is safe to use with children (see page 81, for correct dosage).

Borage
(Borago officinalis)

Burdock, Chickweed, Comfrey and Marigold

These herbs can be made into compresses or ointments to soothe irritated skin.

Comfrey
(Symphytum officinale)

Marigold
(Calendula officinalis)

Psoriasis

Psoriasis is a common skin complaint which has many different causes, ranging from food allergies to stress and shock. It is important to sort out the underlying causes and treat them accordingly. Often sunshine and sea water will clear psoriasis, although this may be only a temporary solution.

Burdock, Cleavers, Sarsaparilla and Yellow Dock

A decoction of these herbs will help cleanse and strengthen the system if taken over a period of time. Dandelion and red clover can also be used.

Skullcap, Motherwort and Lime Blossom

Use one or two of these herbs if there are any symptoms of stress, such as palpitations or high blood pressure. Add them to the burdock, cleavers, sarsaparilla and yellow dock tea.

Comfrey and Chickweed Ointments

Use these externally to help nourish and soften the skin.

ACNE

Acne is a common problem for most adolescents, but it can also continue into later years. Often it is hormonally related which explains its predominance in teenage years and its aggravation before the menstrual cycle. A poor diet of greasy, fried foods or excesses of sugar may also cause an acute attack. These should be avoided and replaced by fresh fruits and vegetables.

Echinacea
(Echinacea angustifolia)

Herbal treatment can be very effective in helping adolescents keep a clear, radiant complexion.

BURDOCK, CLEAVERS, DANDELION, ECHINACEA, RED CLOVER AND YELLOW DOCK

These herbs will help to cleanse the system and clear the skin. Drink one cupful three times a day for at least three weeks.

CHICKWEED, ELDERFLOWER AND MARIGOLD

Combine in equal parts and use as a facial steam.

Red clover
(Trifolium pratense)

EMOTIONS

In today's society there is often pressure to get far too much done in too little time. It is not surprising that stress and anxiety levels are so high, often having physical effects such as headaches, indigestion, backache and many other complaints. Moderate levels of stress and anxiety can turn into chronic depression when people are trapped in situations they feel incapable of changing. People suffering from anxiety, stress or depression for extended periods of time can become tired and unable to cope with the simple tasks of day-to-day life, and they may eventually experience more serious conditions such as nervous exhaustion or a breakdown. Although herbs cannot eradicate the roots of psychological discomfort, they can temporarily alleviate tension, leaving you more relaxed, steadier and brighter – more capable of creating positive changes.

STRESS AND ANXIETY

Stress and anxiety are responses to a difficult situation. Positively, they can help to bring out the best in a person. If the situation does not change, or continues over a long period, the stress of coping with it can be very debilitating. During periods of stress your body uses up nutrients faster than usual. Here are some herbs that will help you to feel stronger and calmer. Use them instead of tea and coffee which contain caffeine.

CHAMOMILE, LIME BLOSSOM, LEMON BALM AND MEADOWSWEET

Drink these herbs instead of coffee or tea to ease any digestive upsets due to nervous tension.

Meadowsweet
(Filipendula ulmaria)

Lemon Balm
(Melissa officinalis)

VERVAIN, SKULLCAP, OATS AND GINSENG

These herbs are general tonics for the nervous system. Taken individually or as a combination, these herbs will help support a person through a stressful period.

Hops
(Humulus lupulus)

Ginseng
(Radix ginseng)

CHAMOMILE, VALERIAN, HOPS AND PASSION-FLOWER

These herbs help ease muscle tension and can be mixed with others for stress, anxiety and depression. Avoid prolonged use of valerian.

DEPRESSION

Depression is another way of reacting to the stresses of life, whether from long-term situations or past causes. Psychotherapy or counselling may help sort out the roots of the problem and provide the individual with the tools to move forward. Exercise, positive self-images, and enjoyable social contacts are also beneficial. If the depression is postnatal or connected with the menstrual cycle include herbs such as agnus castus and wild yam to help balance the hormones. If it occurs after a long illness, use herbs to build up your body.

Lavender
(Lavandula officinalis)

Yoga, positive self-images, and enjoyable social contacts are also beneficial.

GINSENG, LAVENDER, OATS AND ROSEMARY

If the depression is connected with general debility, this mixture of herbs will be beneficial.

Rosemary
(Rosmarinus officinalis)

Borage
(Borago officinalis)

Basil
(Ocimum basilicum)

LEMON BALM, BORAGE, LIME BLOSSOM, BASIL, ST JOHN'S WORT AND SKULLCAP

Any of these herbs can be used on their own or in combination to help brighten the mood.

INSOMNIA

Most people will suffer from an occasional night of disturbed sleep. It can happen at a particularly exciting or stressful time. But when it happens often, or when the worry about going to sleep perpetuates insomnia, it becomes problematic. It can be helpful to establish a routine with regular bedtimes and a relaxing before-bed regime. Avoid stimulating activities in the evening, try a peaceful meditation or some gentle exercise, and substitute relaxing herbal teas for caffeine drinks.

Long Yan Rou (Longan fruit)
Commonly used in China for insomnia associated with overwork and pensiveness. This is a sweet dried fruit similar to raisins which can be eaten or made into a tea. Take 5–15g a day.

SKULLCAP, VALERIAN, PASSION-FLOWER AND HOPS

These herbs can be taken as decoctions, tinctures or pills, and are stronger in their sleep-inducing action, especially in combination with each other. They are useful to break more stubborn patterns of sleeplessness or if pain is causing insomnia.

Avoid prolonged use of valerian, and avoid hops if there are signs of depression.

LEMON BALM, CHAMOMILE, LIME BLOSSOM AND PASSION-FLOWER

These make excellent night-time teas to be drunk in the evening before bed. Lime blossom and chamomile can be made into baths for children (see page 85, in Basic Principles).

SKULLCAP, VALERIAN AND HOPS

These can be made into baths for adults (see page 85, Basic Principles).

Tian Wang Bu Xin Dan
("Emperor of Heaven's special pill to tonify the heart")
This Chinese patent remedy is used for insomnia with restless sleep, irritability, fatigue, short concentration, forgetfulness which may be accompanied by mouth ulcers, night sweats, and constipation. It is especially useful for those who have taken sleeping tablets for so long that they have ceased to be effective. Interestingly, the author of this formula reported that it came to him in a dream from the Emperor of Heaven. In Chinese medicine most sleep disorders are linked with a disturbance in the spirit of the heart, so this is why the heart is mentioned in the English translation of its name.

HYPERACTIVITY

Hyperactivity in children is difficult to define or diagnose. Poor concentration, inability to stay still, and fits of anger or frustration may be symptoms that can be helped by careful diet, patience and a few herbs. Avoid all foods containing artificial colourings, additives and sugars. Avoid over-stimulating activities such as computer games and some television programmes. Encourage physical activities and lots of fresh air.

Fun, outdoor activities can help to ease a child's frustrations and use up excess energy.

RED CLOVER

This herb will be safe to use with children over several months and is useful for clearing the body (some people believe hyperactivity is a result of chemical build-up in the body). It also helps to relax the nerves.

OATS AND VITAMINS C AND B-COMPLEX

These will help repair the nervous system which is under strain due to the hyperactivity.

NERVOUS EXHAUSTION

Nervous exhaustion may occur with long-term emotional conflicts, overwork, the over-consumption of tea, coffee and alcohol, and smoking. During stressful periods vitamins and minerals are used up by the body in higher concentrations. Yet it is often difficult to keep up a healthy diet for various reasons when under stress. You may drink more caffeine and alcohol and smoke more tobacco, all of which cause minerals to be further depleted and put more strain on the body. This may create a destructive cycle as the less energy you have, the less you are able to cope with difficult situations.

If nervous exhaustion reaches an extreme, a collapse or breakdown happens which forces you to rest as part of recovery. Stress, anxiety, depression, insomnia, panic attacks, phobias and overwork may all contribute to nervous exhaustion. Herbs, vitamins C and B-complex, and restful periods can help to fortify the nerves and prevent low vitality.

DANDELION, BURDOCK AND RED CLOVER

These herbs cleanse your system if your diet has been poor or you have consumed large amounts of caffeine or alcohol. Nettles can also be added to help re-mineralize your system. Add relaxing herbs such as vervain or lime blossom if symptoms of stress are present.

Vervain
(Verbena officinalis)

Nervous exhaustion may occur with long-term emotional conflicts, overwork, the over-consumption of tea, coffee and alcohol and smoking.

OATS, VERVAIN, LICORICE AND SKULLCAP

These herbs help to strengthen the nervous system and support the adrenal glands (often these are overtaxed by stress, overwork and caffeine). Drink these herbs at least three times daily while avoiding caffeine, alcohol and tobacco. These are safe to use over a long period.

Astragalus
(Radix astragali membranaceus)

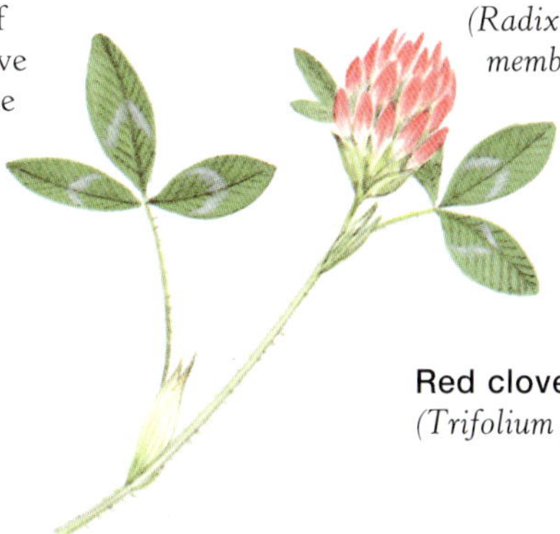

Red clover
(Trifolium pratense)

GINSENG AND ASTRAGALUS

These herbs will help to boost physical energy if there is fatigue as well as nervous exhaustion.

The Bach Flower Remedies

This is a system of 38 remedies made from the flowers of plants, shrubs and trees, almost all of which are found growing wild in Britain. The remedies are prepared by soaking the flowers in spring water and letting them sit in the sun. Other than brandy, which is used to preserve the flowers, no other ingredients are used. Though they are not strictly herbs, they are included in this book because they are also derived directly from plants, and because they are easy and safe to self-prescribe.

Dr Edward Bach

The flower remedies were evolved by Dr Edward Bach, a physician and homeopath, who in 1930 gave up his successful Harley Street practice to develop his healing work using plants.

Dr Edward Bach (1886 - 1936)

It is said that he developed great sensitivity, and that by holding a plant in his hand he had such a strong perception of its energy that he sensed its properties in himself.

How to prescribe

The flower remedies are prescribed according to states of mind, moods and personality traits; it does not follow that they are not effective for physical problems, but rather they can be seen as affecting the body through the mind. Up to six or seven remedies can be mixed together, though they may also be taken singly. The 38 remedies cover a remarkable range of emotional states: they can be used to help someone recover from shock or trauma (see Rescue Remedy, right), give us confidence before interviews or examinations, and even enable us to get over jet-lag more quickly! They are completely safe for old and young, pregnant women, and animals. Plants also benefit from them – never throw away unwanted mixtures of remedies; give them to your plants, which should thrive and flourish as a result!

Preparation and Dosage

10ml dropper bottles of the remedies – known as "stock" bottles – are available from most good chemists, wholefood shops and herbal suppliers. For immediate or emergency use, the remedies should be taken in a small quantity of water, although they may be taken directly from the stock bottle if necessary; this is not recommended for long-term use, however, because of the amount of brandy that the patient will ingest! If you need to take the remedy or remedies over a period of time, obtain a 30ml dropper bottle from a chemist and fill it nearly to the top with still spring water. Add two drops of each of your chosen remedies, and, if you wish, a spoonful of brandy to preserve the mixture. (It will last about three weeks without the brandy, perhaps longer if you keep it in the refrigerator.)

Take four drops at least four times a day, either in a drink or directly on the tongue, taking care not to touch the dropper with your tongue or the mixture may become cloudy as a result. When dealing with intense feelings, you can take the remedies more often: every 15 or 20 minutes is fine.

COMBINATIONS

The most widely known combination of Bach remedies is the Rescue Remedy; it is available already made up in stock bottles from most herbal or wholefood suppliers. It contains five different flower essences: star of Bethlehem, for shock; rock rose, to help deal with panic; impatiens, for tension and impatience; cherry plum, for the fear of losing control; and clematis, to help focus the mind and prevent fainting. Its possible uses are many: after physical or emotional shock, during a panic attack or near-accident, or after receiving bad news. It will calm children waking with night terrors or bad dreams. Rescue Remedy is also available as an ointment, known as Rescue Cream, which is for external use on lesions, rashes, burns etc.

Other combinations are based on individual circumstances, and you will need to mix them up yourself: for jet-lag, for example, try the Rescue Remedy with the addition of walnut (for change) and scleranthus (which is grounding). Keep taking the mixture frequently until you are accustomed to the new time zone. A number of remedies are helpful before tests or interviews: larch builds confidence, white chestnut frees the mind of worrying thought, scleranthus helps with decision-making, aspen keeps fears at bay, and impatiens may prevent you rushing.

As you become familiar with the flower remedies, you will make up your own combinations – the complete safety of this system, even for babies and young animals, means that you can explore its possibilities on yourself, friends and family without risk, as long as you dilute the remedies well for younger patients.

Some people are sceptical about the power of the Bach flower remedies, but herbalists have had some remarkable results through using them, often with people who had not responded to other methods or whose symptoms had become chronic. They work on the level of very subtle energies, which makes their use difficult to subject to laboratory testing, but may also explain their effectiveness.

RESCUE REMEDY

The most widely known combination of Bach remedies. It contains five different flower essences:

Rock rose
– to deal with panic

Star of Bethlehem
– for shock

Impatiens
– for impatience and tension

Cherry plum
– for fear of losing control

Clematis
– to help focus the mind and prevent fainting

THE 38 REMEDIES

AGRIMONY
For those who use a cheerful exterior to disguise their inner pain.

ASPEN
Allays fears which are vague or unconscious in origin; fears of the intangible, or of death.

BEECH
Encourages tolerance in those who are arrogant or critical of others (may be a temporary state).

CENTAURY
For those who feel unassertive, weak-willed or imposed upon by others; this remedy helps them determine and realize what they want.

CERATO
Relates to inner certainty; helps people who doubt their own judgement and constantly seek advice.

CHERRY PLUM
Provides reassurance for those who feel they may be on the verge of a breakdown, or "going out of my mind".

CHESTNUT BUD
Helps people to learn by their mistakes; for those who find it hard to become wiser through experience, or who repeat old patterns.

CHICORY
Enables you to let go: for those who are over-possessive of loved ones.

CLEMATIS
Aids concentration in those that are dreamy, unfocused or vague.

CRAB APPLE
Known as "the cleanser"; helpful for shame, negative feelings about self, after rape or abuse. Often effective for hay fever or rhinitis.

ELM
Relates to responsibility; helpful for those who take on more than they can deal with, and become overwhelmed.

GENTIAN
Restores faith in the process of life. Useful for despondency or depression, when the cause is known.

GORSE
Restores hope for those who have given up; despair or chronic illness may be part of the picture.

HEATHER
For those obsessed with their own problems; helps develop compassion.

HOLLY
For rage, jealousy, anger, or any negative emotion; paradoxically, it also helps you contact your true feelings when you feel "cut off".

HONEYSUCKLE
For those nostalgic for the past, honeysuckle will enable letting go and embracing the present.

HORNBEAM
Restores energy when you feel temporarily unmotivated, or procrastinate; often called the "Monday morning" remedy.

IMPATIENS
For impatience and irritability; people who find it hard to work in a team because of these qualities may benefit.

LARCH
Enhances self-confidence and helps you overcome feelings of inferiority or fear of failure.

MIMULUS
Helps deal with fears of known or tangible things, gives courage in the case of phobias.

MUSTARD
Helps reinstate optimism in people who experience sudden depression without a known cause.

OAK
Relates to strength and endurance; for those who over-achieve or set themselves impossibly high goals.

OLIVE
Regenerates peace and balance after long periods of overwork or emotional exhaustion.

PINE
Helps you to forgive yourself; useful for those with an over-developed sense of guilt.

RED CHESTNUT
Relates to compassion and solicitude; helpful for people who are obsessive about their concern for others, to the point where they project all their own fears onto them.

ROCK ROSE
Reassures where there is panic, terror, or sudden alarm.

ROCK WATER
Not actually a flower, but derived from spring water in natural locations, this remedy frees up people who keep themselves under rigid self-control or self-denial.

SCLERANTHUS
Grounding, helps us make decisions and allays uncertainty or mood swings.

STAR OF BETHLEHEM
Reassures after shock or trauma, sudden loss or accident.

SWEET CHESTNUT
Helps release the user from a state of hopeless despair.

VERVAIN
Restores balance to the person who expends energy in over-enthusiasm or fanatical beliefs; has a gentle sedative action.

VINE
Relates to qualities of authority and leadership; in the negative vine state, a person may be controlling, ruthless, and power-hungry.

WALNUT
A protective remedy, helping you through periods of transition or gateways; walnut facilitates change.

WATER VIOLET
Relates to humility – indications include withdrawn behaviour, deliberate isolation – the person is reserved and proud.

WHITE CHESTNUT
Dispels persistent unwanted thoughts; often used for insomnia.

WILD OAT
Helps people find their true direction, purpose or career, and thus fulfilment.

WILD ROSE
Recreates motivation for those who are apathetic or resigned.

WILLOW
Helps give you a sense of personal responsibility: someone in a negative willow frame of mind feels bitter, like a victim, and blames others.

Consulting a Herbal Practitioner

Having developed an interest in herbs, you may wish to enlist the advice and experience of a qualified herbalist; or you may find your health problem is beyond the scope of this book. (Potentially serious ailments, such as asthma, tumours or heart conditions, have not been included because obviously these require the attention of a professional). You should also bear in mind that some herbs, like some foods, may cause an allergic reaction in sensitive people; if you experience new symptoms while taking herbs, you are strongly recommended to consult a reputable practitioner who will be able to identify the problem. You may be lucky enough to find a herbalist through someone who can recommend a practitioner; it is generally reassuring to know something about their reputation and the way they work. Otherwise, you will need to contact one of the organizations which keep registers of practitioners. For Western herbalists in the UK, try the National Institute of Medical Herbalists, whose address is given opposite.

If you are feeling adventurous (or maybe just out of curiosity) of if your condition is more serious, you may prefer to consult someone qualified in prescribing Chinese herbs, in which case the organization to contact is the Register of Chinese Herbal Medicine (see page 123).

Chinese herbs have a well-deserved reputation for tasting unpleasant (though this is not always the case), but they are more powerful and therefore sometimes more effective than Western herbs.

What to expect

Most herbalists will take a fairly detailed case history, and if you have not consulted a complementary therapist before, this can come as something of a surprise. You may wonder why they need to know about the activities of your bowels, if you have consulted them about your psoriasis! The answer, of course, is that herbalists mostly work in a holistic way, and need to know as much about the workings of your body and mind as possible, in order to determine what is amiss with your energy.

In Chinese medicine, groups of apparently unrelated symptoms are known as syndromes or "patterns of disharmony", and your practitioner will need to identify how this theoretical framework applies to you; this will generally involve taking your pulse and looking at your tongue, both of which provide a valuable source of information about your energy. Many people in Western cultures are a little shy about showing their tongue to a comparative stranger; rest assured that the herbalist is not trying to identify what you had for breakfast, but is looking at the colour, shape and coating of your tongue to help determine a correct diagnosis.

Having prescribed a suitable mixture of herbs for you, the practitioner will either mix up the prescription in tincture form for immediate use, or (more likely with Chinese herbs) write out a prescription for you to obtain. Sometimes the herbalist will send the list of herbs to a herbal supplier to be mixed up and posted to you, or occasionally you may be given the herbs in powder, tablet or tincture form. If you live in London and your herbalist can write in Chinese characters, you may have the amazing experience of going to one of the Chinese herbal shops in Soho, where you can sit and wait, surrounded by jars of extraordinary-looking substances, while the assistant weighs out each of your herbs in hand-held scales and wraps them up in paper. The herbs will need decocting daily; follow the instructions for preparation given you by your herbal practitioner. Unlike Western herbs, Chinese herbs are often decocted twice, so that each packet of herbs lasts two days.

If the herbs are not working...

Firstly, have a close look at your lifestyle and diet to see if there are any bad habits blocking the herbs from doing their job. It is simply unrealistic to expect the subtle, natural energy of herbs to have an effect if you live on hamburgers, never exercise, and smoke 40 cigarettes a day! This is an extreme example of course, but it cannot be over emphasized that herbs work best in a body which is also cared for in other ways. It may be helpful, for instance, to consult a nutritionist to help work out a good diet and supplement any vitamin or mineral deficiencies you may have.

Secondly, it will be harder for the herbs to work if the energy is blocked somewhere in your body, or if important structures are out of alignment. Seeing an acupuncturist or osteopath can make an enormous difference.

Lastly, it will be difficult to relieve symptoms which are the result of unresolved emotions; if this is the case, you should find a good counsellor or therapist so that you can deal with any emotional blocks, enabling your energy to respond more freely to the herbs.

USEFUL ADDRESSES

REGISTERS OF PRACTITIONERS AND HEALTH INFORMATION

Register of Chinese Herbal Medicine
PO Box 400
Wembley
Middlesex HA9 9NZ
Tel: 020 8904 1357

British Association for Counselling
37a Sheep Street
Rugby CV21 3BX
Tel: 01788–578328

The Bach Centre
Mount Vernon
Sotwell
Wallingford
Oxon OX10 0PZ
Tel: 01491–839489

School of Meditation
158 Holland Park Avenue
London W11 4UH
Tel: 020 7603 6116

Women's Health Information Centre
52 Featherstone Street
London EC1Y 8RT
Tel: 020 7251 6580

Society for the Promotion
of Dietary Therapy
PO Box 47
Heathfield
East Sussex TN21 8ZX
Tel: 01435–867007

Register of Traditional
Chinese Medicine
19 Trinity Road
London N2 8JH
Tel: 010 8883 8431

Council for Acupuncture
179 Gloucester Place
London NW1 6DX
Tel: 020 7724 5756

The Society of Homeopaths
2 Artizan Road
Northampton NN1 4HU
Tel: 01604–21400

General Council and
Register of Osteopaths
56 London Street
Reading RG1 4SQ
Tel: 01734–576585

National Institute of
Medical Herbalists
9 Palace Gate
Exeter EX1 1JA
Tel: 01392–426022

HERBAL SUPPLIERS

FOR WESTERN HERBS:

Baldwins Health Food Centre
171–173 Walworth Road
London SE17 1RW
Tel: 020 7703 5550

East-West Herbs
Langston Priory Mews
Kingham
Oxon OX7 6UP
Tel: 01608–658862
Fax: 01608–658816

East-West Herb Shop
3 Neal's Yard
London WC2H 9DP
Tel: 020 7379 1312

Neal's Yard Apothecary
2 Neal's Yard
Covent Garden
London WC2H 9DP
Tel: 020 7379 7222

Potters Ltd
Leyland Mill Lane
Wigan
Lancashire WN1 2SB
Tel: 01942 34761

Phytoproducts
Tidebrook Manor Farm
Wadhurst
Sussex TN5 6PD

FOR CHINESE HERBS:

Acu-Medic
101–105 Camden High Street
London NW1 7JN
Tel: 020 7388 6704

East-West Herbs (see left)

Mayway (UK) Ltd
Waterside Trading Estate
Trumpers Way
Hanwell W7 2QD
Tel: 020 8893 6873
Fax: 020 8893 6874

Harmony
Acupuncture
Supplies
629 High Road
Leytonstone
London E11 4PA
Tel: 020 8518 7337
Fax: 020 8518 7338

Reading List

Although this book lists about one hundred herbs, it is intended only as an introduction. If you want to develop your knowledge of herbs and Bach flower remedies, the following books are recommended:

Barnard, J. &M., *The Healing Herbs of Edward Bach* (Bach Educational Programme, Hereford, 1988).
Bach, Dr. E., *The Twelve Healers and Other Remedies* (C.W. Daniel, Essex). Describes all 38 flower remedies.

Bensky, D. and Barlott, R., *Chinese Herbal Medicine – Formulas and Strategies* (Eastland Press, 1990).

Bensky, D., and Gamble, A., *Chinese Herbal Medicine – Materia Medica* (Eastland Press, Washington, 1986).

Campion, K., *A Woman's Herbal* (Century, London, 1987).

Curtis, S., Fraser, R., and Kohler, I., *Neal's Yard Natural Remedies* (Arkana, London, 1988).

Fratkin, J., *Chinese Herbal Patent Formulas* (Institute for Traditional Medicine, Portland, Oregon). Rather detailed for the beginner, but very thorough.

Grieve, Mrs. M., *A Modern Herbal* (Penguin Books, London, 1989).

Hoffman, D., *The Holistic Herbal* (Element, Dorset, 1983). Essential reading for every herbal user.

Lust, J., *The Herb Book* (Bantam, New York, 1986).
This American herbal lists a vast range of herbs, though some which grow in the UK; also a useful list of suppliers in the US.

McIntyre, A., *The Herbal for Mother and Child* (Element, Dorset, 1992).

McIntyre, A., *Herbs for Common Ailments* (Gaia Books, London, 1992). Beautifully illustrated and highly recommended.

Scheffer, M., *Bach Flower Therapy – Theory and Practice* (Thorsons, Northants, 1986). A very clear and positive guide to the flower remedies.

INDEX

Note: Page numbers in *italics* refer to illustrations

Acknowledgements

Key: a=above b=below l=left r=right
E.T. Archive 7; Ken Scott/Tony Stone Images 9; Harry Smith Horticultural Collection 11, 12, 14a, 15al, 16a, 19a, 20al, 21a; Mauritius/Ace 43; Pictor 45; Tibor Bognor/Ace 48; Chris Harvey/Tony Stone Images 49; Nawrocki Stock Photos/Ace 50; David Le Lossy/Image Bank 54b; Simon Wilkinson/Image Bank 55; Pictor 56; Gabe Palmer/Ace 58; Auschromes/Ace 59a; David Le Lossy/Image Bank 60; Hulton-Deutsch Collection 66; John MacRae-Brown/Ace 67; E.T. Archive 68; Harry Smith Horticultural Collection 76r, 77r & 78r; John Searle/Ace 79r; Image Bank 82r; Max Schnider/Image Bank 83br; Bard Martin/Image Bank 110bl; Zephyr Pictures/Ace 111r; Pictor 113ar; David Vance/Image Bank 115ar; Eric Simmons/Image Bank 116; Pictor 117a, a courtesyof the Dr. E Bach Centre 118b.

Quarto would like to thank the Tisserand Institute, East Sussex, for their assistance, and Marle Place Garden & Nursery, Kent, for supplying form of the herbs uses on photography.

Author's Acknowledgements
Anna Selby would like to dedicate her work to Christian; Tamara Kircher would like to thank her children, Ryan and Molly Jo for their interest, understanding and self-sufficiency and Clive for his patience and his computer, and Penny Lowery would like to thank Claire Grey for the loan of books and Eileen Bonner for her patience and her computer!

Jacket design by Rod Teasdale.
Index by Dorothy Frame.